Women, Walking

WOMEN, WALKING

CONTEMPORARY VOICES ON NATURE AND BELONGING

Kerri Andrews

BATSFORD

First published in the United Kingdom in 2026 by
Batsford
43 Great Ormond Street
London
WC1N 3HZ

An imprint of B. T. Batsford Holdings Limited

ISBN 9781837330683

A CIP catalogue record for this book is available from the British Library.

10 9 8 7 6 5 4 3 2 1

Reproduction by Rival Colour Ltd, UK

Printed and bound by Dream Colour, China

This book can be ordered direct from the publisher at www.batsfordbooks.com, or try your local bookshop.

Distributed throughout the UK and Europe by Abrams & Chronicle Books, 1st Floor, 22–24 Ely Place, London EC1N 6TE and 57 rue Gaston Tessier, 75166 Paris, France

www.abramsandchronicle.co.uk
info@abramsandchronicle.co.uk

For Fhionnlagh and Beth.

It's all for you, always.

Contents

Introduction

Kerri Andrews

Stories and paths are not that different, if you think about it. When we tell a story we are bringing into the world a fragment of human experience that can be shared, understood, commiserated over, retold. Storytelling is how tradition and knowledge and emotion are passed on, down and around. And so too with paths. They are stories in their own way, communicating where people have trodden, how often and perhaps even why. As we pass along the paths we encounter, adding the impression of our feet to the countless number that came before us, we join their stories. We *become* their stories. And, as we walk, as we remake the path anew, we ensure they remain open for the next person, the next generation. Stories and paths are, I think, two connected kinds of history: evidence that we were here, that we made an impression.

For many of us, writing – or drawing, or composing, or creating in a multitude of meaningful ways – and walking are deeply connected. Walking offers for many people a way to access that inner wellspring of creativity, quieting the din of everyday life and its endless concerns and chatter so that something deeper can come to the fore. Afoot we cannot help but touch the more-than-human world, a world that is ready to transport us beyond human concerns, beyond ourselves. The path is a place the mind can come untethered.

Walking isn't a cure for anything, not the modern condition nor a long-term illness, but it is a way of returning ourselves to our bodies, to the core of who we are. It doesn't have to be far, and it doesn't have to be up, for us to benefit from movement outside, from the pleasure of feeling our bodies make contact with the earth.

That the benefits and pleasures of walking have not, and are not, available to all is a central concern to this collection. Walking literature has tended to take for granted that walking is vigorous and energetic and equalising. Writers who are considered to embody these ideas have tended to receive the most acclaim, people like William Wordsworth and Henry Thoreau, Raynor Winn and Cheryl Strayed, Robert Macfarlane and Bill Bryson. Anthologies and collections about walking repeat the pattern, and add others: the names that come up again and again are too often male, white and living in bodies that exist without impediments like chronic illness or childbearing or caring. But what about writers who don't match this description? Bodies coded as female have often been written out of walking history altogether, had written onto them particular stories, or been restricted to just a few paths. This collection looks to break these old patterns by giving much overdue and well-earned space to writers living with disability and chronic illness, writers of colour, who are trans, who live in bodies that shift in composition and meaning as they move in time and space.

Indeed, the value of walking is not singular, or even necessarily quantifiable. It is subjective, fleeting, dependent on circumstances that flash in and out of existence or relevance. Walking's value to creativity depends in no small degree on the contexts in which it is undertaken and encountered. And there, too, walking and storytelling overlap, because what could be more subjective than story? We bring to stories, and take meaning from them, much that is personal to us in this moment. Tomorrow, or next week, when we don't have that deadline, or the rain isn't pouring, or we haven't just come from a loved one's bedside, our story, or the path, will look and feel utterly different. There is no right way to walk. There is no right way to tell a story. There are just the ways that feel right: in this moment; in this way.

This collection includes ten very different pieces of work. They have all responded to the same guidance: to consider why walking matters to creativity, but they have each taken their own, often meandering, routes; they have chosen different directions, tackled different terrain. But they all share a fundamental belief: that walking is vital to how we think of ourselves as human beings and as artists.

The variety of approaches demonstrates the rich possibilities of walking literature when it is unshackled from the limiting tropes of walking-as-heroism, or walking-as-conquering. Some of the writers included here describe grand adventures and big peaks, but not as places to test themselves (and win). Instead, they prize places where their stories and those of the land can intermingle.

The contributors here bring a wide range of experiences in terms of body, social class and ethnic origin. Some of the writing is combative: about the restrictions imposed by the old shibboleths of walking literature; about societal expectations; about the shortcomings of our storytelling. The pieces here challenge not only who has been able to write about walking, but the range of meanings walking has been allowed to have. Other essays offer consolation or inspiration, and alternative paths through life are revealed. Different stories become possible.

For Josie Giles, whose piece 'Cruachan Beann' opens the collection, walking makes clear the power dynamics at play when we set foot in the hills, from the observations we make of others' bodies, to the politics of the land we tread. Her essay is lyrically excoriating, outlining as it does our complicity in draining the land of meaning. In her writing, the land is re-storied, re-peopled.

Polly Atkin's essay also offers an alternative story, one where disability and chronic illness are not overwritten by stories of recovery and adventure, but are allowed to co-exist. As Polly demonstrates, there is a long and rich history of walking and disability that can, and should, be recognised: not separately, but as part of the larger story of walking.

Overlapping stories feature too in Anita Sethi's piece, as she walks through late-night Manchester and finds a land of politics and complex history subsumed beneath the facade of modernity. Simultaneously exploring Manchester's streets and waterways and its dark and poorly remembered complicity in slavery and indentured servitude, Anita demonstrates how walking can help bring forward what others might wish to forget.

Remembering is central to Beatrice Searle's beautiful essay that shows how walking can reconcile past and present, trauma and healing, the gap between generations. In what is, ultimately, a love letter to her mother, Beatrice weaves together the ancient history of Northumberland's coastal rocks with the history of her own family, and shows how sharing a path can open the possibility of a new story.

Family and the delights of walking locally also concern Gail Simmons. Having written before about the joy of long-distance routes, Gail in this piece offers an exploration of the meaning and wonder inherent in the kind of walking so many of us do: in familiar places, along familiar paths, season after season after season. There is sadness in this kind of walking, Gail finds, as things change and are lost. But there is hope and comfort too, in walking again the paths we have loved and finding in that meaning and connection with what has gone. Linda Cracknell's essay offers an alternative view of how we might connect with what has past, as she sets off through a storied but no longer peopled landscape in Perthshire on an unusual journey, a 'shopping holiday'.

Katharine Norbury, Anna Fleming and Helen Mort take on more directly the challenge to connect walking with creativity. Katharine shows us how now and in the past walking has helped creative people find the 'magical places' where the world of the imagination and the physical world overlap, collide and merge. She takes us from the enchanted woods of Shakespeare's *A Midsummer Night's Dream* to the similarly wondrous landscapes of north Wales, where pilgrims came in their thousands to find, and perhaps touch, the divine. Katharine shows us how these different places and different worlds draw together for us as we walk.

For Anna Fleming, walking is part of the work of writing, an essential path into the most creative parts of her mind. In her piece Anna takes us on a guided tour through Edinburgh along urban paths and fleeting green space. But gradually being overlaid on the walk is another topography, one of mind and imagination: the paths Anna treads with her feet open up routes inwards into the wellspring of creativity. Nor is this some rarefied place: this inner sanctum of focus and awareness can be found by anyone willing to follow this road along and within.

In her essay Helen Mort shows us how walking and the writing of poetry coincide and coexist. But she also writes about the lies we tell (ourselves, each other, you) about how writing and walking interlink. With lyrical honesty Helen breaks down the blind spots of her own creative practice of linking walking and writing, while opening up to view what has too often been wilfully ignored about the realities of walking as a woman – menstruation not least among them.

And in the closing piece of the collection, the drumbeat of 'walking cure' is the deserved target of Kate Davis's ridicule and anger. Lambasting the glossy TV shows and magazine pieces that insist on the 'wellness' effects of walking, Kate shows how high production values are unable to cover up that walking cannot bring about 'wellness': no number of miles covered can rewrite genetics or cow misfiring cells into submission. It is a strident rebuttal of some of the most damaging tropes of walking literature and walking shows, and is a fitting conclusion to a collection that seeks to demolish for good the old ways of writing about walking.

Cruachan Beann

Harry Josephine Giles

At six in the morning, with blue dawn easing over tenement roofs, I load up the car with gear: leather and polyester, nylon and carbon fibre, PFAS and protein bars. I hurl through the empty streets and up the open M9, burning my share of hydrocarbons to haste me to the Highland Boundary Fault. My route leads over rising land, past Loch Lùdnaig, where the hills and woods begin to gather, through Gleann Dochart, thick with Sitka, and past the hikers' capitals of a' Chrion-Làraich, the withered place, and Taigh an Droma, the house on the ridge. The straights and turns are familiar to me, the gear shifts, the public toilets and the places where traffic thickens. A dozen or so times a year I'm on this road to the western hills. All my spending of time and carbon is for this, to take me again up a mountain.

Today my mountain is Cruachan Beann, a granite massif in the far west, sitting between Loch Obha and Loch Èite, dammed valley-steward, bare-headed pass-watcher, the last great height before the crossing to Muile.

Here is a horseshoe of peaks set around a reservoir, an eight-hour trek even for my long legs, a well-known hike I've saved for a day like this: still, warm, clear, blue.

I pull my little red car into the rank of beasts unsociably crowding the verge of the A85, churning up spring mud. The parking is prohibited but unpoliced, too many making the same choice for anyone to enforce otherwise, and besides, if we weren't here then we'd be bothering the village or the power station. We're all here together imagining the mountain.

Why the mountain? To shake my bones. To see what I see. To win the summit. To learn the landscape. To be alone in my thoughts, away from signal and all it carries. To make connections. To make use of my body. To be free of any duty but the next step. But each step on the path around the mountain, walking between one thing and the other, along the watershed between Obha and Èite, along the property boundary between Castles Estate Ltd and the Maitlands' Glenoe, is a step along the lines of power and language. I write as I walk, and when the one view leaves, the next view appears. Why the mountain? Because the mountain holds me in my world.

Obha, known as Awe, is a vowel shift from Abha, and Abha a contraction from Abhainn's ancestor: 'river', spoken in Avon and Abhainn and Afon and in each of their descendants. Once, the people who depended on the Obha knew it only as the river, definitive, and then as a sound that suggested river, and then as a sound washed smooth into only a memory of water: oh, oh, oh, ah, ah, ah. And then another people came, as they do, and asked what the river was called, and the old people said 'river', and the new people said their word for water just a little differently, and the river became Abhainn Obha, the river river. And then another people came, as they do, whose words for water flowed from another source, and when they were told the name of the river they heard what they felt: Awe.

Above the Awe is Cruachan Beann. 'Beinn' is peak, and so is 'cruach', but each shades different, making the name less a doubling and more a specification. Beinn is often but not always the highest mountain, often but not always the whole collection of peaks, often but not always paired with greatness, mòr. Scotland is pinned in English by Ben Mores and Morvens. What's the name of that mountain? Oh, that's the big hill. Cruach is less common and more precise, the name for a haystack or anything that looks like a haystack, towering and tapering. Like stob and stuc and sgùrr, each a peak of their own with their own shape, cruach gives a clear direction by which to navigate as you walk beside the Awe. Where am I going? Oh, follow the river until the pointy peak comes into view, then turn south around the red hill; keep an eye out for the cliff where the eagles nest, and then walk towards the rock that looks like an old woman's nose. You can't miss it. So: Cruachan Beann and Abhainn Obha, the peak of peaks watching over the water water.

*

My first steps are up the steep sides of the glen, just above the water that flows from the mountain, through oak and birch. The birches are silver and slim, crowding the path, their buds just now opening into neat little leaves. It's not yet nine but there's already heat in the day, and I haven't stretched my calves enough after their work on accelerator and clutch.

Leaning on sticks to steady my breath, I find I'm next to an astonishment: a granny oak, twisted and leaning over the water, her arms wide to keep the young birches in their place. She's home to mosses and lichens I can't name, and dark drips run down her trunk. She has the brutal clarity of every creature that's older than I can ever be, and as much disregard for me as I've regard for her. To me, she's persistence, bloody-mindedly binding the bank of the burn, seeing her way through waves of felling and planting, keeping her leaves far enough from deer and sheep to know the sun. To the mountain, whose heights I can't yet spy, she's an itch to scratch. I move on.

On Cruachan Beann lived an old woman whose name was Sharp, with white hair and blue skin and one keen eye. She made the mountains for her stepping stones and carved the valleys with swings of her frost-rimed hammer. At the highest peak of all the peaks was a well, and every night the sharp old woman would cover the well with a slab, and every morning she would let the water loose again. But one night she was so tired from herding her deer all up and down the slopes of Cruachan Beann that she fell asleep beside the open well. The waters overflowed and rushed down into the valleys towards the sea, making the river and the loch known now by the name of Awe.

I lip the corrie, carved by a glacier a few millennia back, into a high wet field that smells of dung. The sheep hum. At first the dam in the mountain's belly looks only like an old dyke, a low tumble of black stones, the kind of work I could see my own hands doing. But as I lumber over the gravel and around the puddles, the dam rises higher and grows to stretch from one flank of the mountain to the other. Its wide buttresses are black teeth biting down into the bowl of the valley. It seems now a thing impossible to build, a thing summoned by a spell, by a giant's will, by mouse-click and sparkle. But it too was made by men laying one stone on top of another until they were done. As I come closer, the dam's black walls shrink again into something I can see, with rough stones and rust stains. It has texture and smell: cheesegrater and rockblood. I open the steel gate where dam meets earth and it whines like a dog. My feet on the gantry sing over the glassy reservoir.

The Cruachan power station was built by the state, or rather built by workers employed by the state, thirty-six of whom died in its making, or rather its making killed them. The dam used new night-time nuclear energy to pump water up through the turbines and into the reservoir, and then let that water fall all through the day to make more power. Water and electricity flowed in a cycle across the country and through the mountain. Now Hunterston A, the nuclear power station built at the same time, has fallen still, waiting fifty more years to be felled, and the water keeps flowing through the mountain. Now the power station built by workers has been sold by the state to a private company, and the water keeps flowing through the mountain.

This dam these days is owned by Drax, which takes its name from a wood-burning power station, which takes its name from a village in Yorkshire. The website of Drax Global describes the company as 'shaping tomorrow's energy landscape'. In the header image are three cooling towers which look as clean and white as wind turbines. Below the towers are a picture of a pine forest, a picture of five children in blue jumpers playing with Lego next to a computer tablet, a picture of children in plastic outdoor clothes walking down a path strewn with autumn's brown and black and gold. 'Our purpose,' says the website, 'is to enable a zero carbon, lower cost energy future.'

Drax sources 80 per cent of the wood it burns from old growth forests in North America, from Indigenous land unceded or governed by miskept treaties. Drax ships the granny pines across the Atlantic as pellets for burning, and claims this process is carbon neutral, releasing only what was gained as the trees grew. This status allows the incinerator to reap renewable energy subsidies. Notwithstanding how long it took the pines to store that carbon, the ancient ecosystem they fostered is not renewable: that web of human and more-than-human relations is shrinking by the day. In 2024 Drax was fined £25 million after the energy regulator found that it had submitted inaccurate data on its wood sourcing. They could not truly say how many old pines they had burned.

*

Cruachan Beann holds a mirror in her hands. Once the glass was only the glacier's leavings, a little lochan whose rough shape now is drowned. These days the greater waters rise and fall with the moon and the sun, with the pouring out of power through the hollow mountain's turbines. Here, in the reservoir, on this windless day, each of the peaks has its partner, the one pointing up to the hidden stars, the other pointing down to the centre of the Earth, with not a ripple to say which is which.

Inside Cruachan Beann lives an old woman whose name is Sharp, made of brown wood and black plastic and gold gold. Six feet tall, she crawls with her slab, always in the act of opening or closing the well. She was made in London by a woman whose name was Falconer, a work of art for a hall of power. Behind her in space and after her in time are the graves of workers and the sculpted torrent of pouring water. From the hollow mountain, a net of wires and pylons and substations holds the country together, powering the laptop on which I write, the server which holds the data for my weather forecast, the phone by which I navigate up the mountain.

There are men's voices behind me as I rise up the corrie's flank. There often are. They're only laughing, but my body responds to laughing men with fear. They're doing me no harm, but my memory hears a threat. Every few minutes I check their pace and find it the same as mine.

The way sound carries on a hill, their laughter will be behind me all the way, but if I let them by, then I won't hear another word. I pull to the side of the path and sip my water until they reach me. As they come close, their conversation drops. We nod to each other, all aware of our breathlessness. 'Morning,' I say, naming what's passing.

Sometimes men's eyes linger on me, making their assessment. Sometimes they slip by, afraid to look, afraid of what might look back. I see my body through their eyes: six feet tall, sweaty, rock-scraped, miscurved, between shapes. The mountain responds to the pressure of my feet and my sticks, meeting the weight of my body: she does not look, and so with her I forget my looks until another human sees me. I let the four men pass, watching the muscles of their calves contract and expand, hearing their laughter fade away into the future.

In the *Star Wars* television series *Andor*, the Ben Cruachan dam, its English name flipping the grammar of the Gaelic, plays an imperial base on the planet Aldhani. A rebel cell hikes over the planet's hills to steal the base's gold. When I see the dam I remember the mission. Diego Luna plays the Andor of the title, a cynical thief who takes a long journey to become the hero that saves the galaxy as the Rebel Alliance grows from underground movement to insurgent military force. *Andor* was produced by Disney+, a service owned by Disney Streaming, which is the streaming division of Disney Entertainment, which is a business segment of the Walt Disney Corporation. With a revenue of over $90 billion dollars, Disney was in 2025 the second biggest media corporation in the world. The dam is owned by Drax, 2 per cent of which is owned by Bank of America (sixth largest corporation at $197bn), 5 per cent by Blackrock (191st, $21bn) and 9 per cent by Invesco (1,620th, $6bn).

I asked ChatGPT how much Disney payed Drax to use the Ben Cruachan dam. The chatbot tells me emphatically, with this note in bold, that Disney did not pay Drax, but that instead Drax made charitable donations 'running to five figures' to local causes: the restoration of St Conan's Kirk, a local defibrillator network, and a vehicle for Oban Mountain Rescue, the people who would find me if I fell. ChatGPT linked to a source for this claim, a BBC news article. On examination, I found that the article did not in fact state whether or not Disney payed Drax: ChatGPT processed the BBC article, which processed a press release from Drax, and decided that the absence of evidence that Drax was paid was evidence that Drax was not paid. ChatGPT is a naive intepreter of corporate press statements.

Some estimates suggest that my question to ChatGPT consumed the equivalent of a bottle of water. The latest press statement by ChatGPT's owner, OpenAI (revenue: $3.7bn), claims the question consumed only a teaspoon or two.

It's a hard push to the highest summit of Cruachan Beann: the grassy side of the corrie turns to steep rock slope, the good path turns to great stones. The heat of the day is rising and sweat is running down my bra. There's no way to take the small steps needed to save energy for a long day in the hills: my hamstrings tauten, my arms brace and pull on boulders. My long hair has slipped from its tie and is slicked to my brow. I haul myself up to the cairn. A dozen or so walkers sit quietly in the sun, each pair or trio minding their own view. I recognise a few from when they passed me on the climb. 'Oh aye,' I say, smiling. 'Here's everybody.' Nobody speaks.

Each summit has its own moods, varying by the day. Easier, grassier summits tend to conversation, to walkers sharing their greetings and memories. Distant summits offer solitude, rarely seeing more than one human at once. The most popular summits on the sunniest days tend to quiet. Is it that everyone's too tired to speak? Is it that I, rangy and alone, am too strange a vision to speak to? Or is it that everyone came for quiet and found a crowd?

In the *Guardians of the Galaxy* films, a series in the Marvel Cinematic Universe, the former professional wrestler Dave Bautista plays Drax the Destroyer. Red scarification covers his smoothly muscled grey body. He speaks literally, without comprehension of sarcasm or metaphor. In this he is comic relief, a mountain of a man who makes laughter because he doesn't know what he's saying. Drax's homeworld was invaded by imperial forces and half his people were killed: in all the films, he is the only one of his people we meet, the only one who speaks his language. Like Andor, he is a fugitive and a refugee fighting half for revenge and half to save the galaxy from imperial violence. The Marvel Cinematic Universe is distinct from the Star Wars Expanded Universe, but both are owned by the Disney Corporation.

Here, at the height, the view: skyline after skyline, mountains layered one behind the other, blueing themselves under this bright sun. The humid air fades each after each, so that every mountain further into the future becomes less mountain, more sky. I give them their names and greet them as friends.

DRAX is also the name of the Walt Disney Corporation's advertising business, the Disney Real-Time Ad Exchange, which enables the buying and selling of adverts across Disney properties. Various press releases explain how Disney's advertising business is integrated with the major corporations of our time. In 2024, they say that Disney 'announced agreements with Google's DV360 and The Trade Desk, significantly simplifying how advertisers access premium inventory across Disney's streaming platforms', which 'strengthens Disney's position in the evolving streaming advertising landscape, by connecting Disney's Real-Time Ad Exchange (DRAX) directly to DSPs'. In 2025 they 'integrated with Amazon's Demand-Side Platform (Amazon DSP)', thus 'building a direct path connecting Amazon's commerce insights to the full scale of Disney's streaming ecosystem' and 'enabling greater accessibility to inventory and audience signals'. I don't know what any of these words mean. The Forbes Global 2000 tells me that Google's revenue, trading as

Alphabet, is $359bn, placing it ninth, and that Amazon's is $638bn, placing it fifth. I adblock my browser and thief all my television so that I do not have to see any of the adverts they sell. Who topped the list? Who was first up the mountain?

Below the peak, sitting at a thousand metres, is a rough step, tilted protrusions of black granite refusing all pathmaking. Here it's hand on rock and careful choices. I know from other hills that the mountain likes a confident grip: hesistant steps are unstable; sweaty hands slip; limbs at full extension are liable to cramp. As long as I don't believe I am afraid, I can swing easily from hold to hold with little chance of falling. But as soon as I acknowledge that this hill could shrug me off without thinking, could toss me tumbling down the slope to smash into the mirror, I'm stuck, suspended, arms and legs spreadeagled against black rock, unable to go forward or back. I close my eyes and put my cheek to the hill. 'You can do this,' I say, to either myself or the stones. 'You've done it before. You'll do it again.' And I've done it, I do it, I will do it. I'm over the rocks and on the ridge, and soon I've forgotten there was ever a danger.

James Drax was one of the earliest English settlers of Barbados. In 1642, having established a sugar plantation of some four hundred acres, he bought twenty-two enslaved humans, and thirty-four more two years later. He led the economic model of plantation slavery which shaped the islands and the world. His descendant,

Richard Drax, was the Conservative MP for Dorset until 2024, and owns at least 5,600 hectares of farmland and woodland, making him likely the largest landowner in Parliament. In 2023 the government of Barbados initiated plans to demand reparations from the Drax family. So far Richard Drax has refused. In Barbados, Drax Hall still stands, surrounded by planted sugarcane.

I think: I love this mountain. 'I love this,' I say as I walk, but not, 'I love you.' The mountain speaks in pipit and tumbling pebble, in grey dust and cooling breeze. I try to understand her words. What responsibility do we owe to each other in love?

In the waulking song 'Dh'Èirich Mise, Rinn Mi Gluasad', words shaped by centuries of women workers, a woman combs her long hair beside the well on Cruachan Beann and remembers the man who has abandoned her and the mountain for the city and another lover.

In the love song ''S Toigh Leam an Tè Dhìleas Dhonn', too old to have an author, a man away travelling remembers his love who lives by Cruachan Beann, fearing she'll be married before he's home.

In the praise song 'Duanag do Chruachan Beann', by Pàdraig Mac an t-Saoir, the exiled singer praises the mountain above all others, and laments that he can never return ''S bhon a chuir iad thu fo fhèidh', since they put you under deer.

In the protest song 'An Caochladh Truagh', by Gilleasbaig MacIain, are the lines:

Beinn-Cruachan fèin is guirme snuadh,
Bidh 'cridh' fo chràdh ri tuireadh truagh,
A chionn 's nach cluinn i chaoidh gu buan
Ach goileam cruaidh nan Sasannach.

(Cruachan Beann herself has the bluest look / sorry lamentation breaks her heart / because she will never again hear / anything but harsh English babble)

All the sounds gather to the velum, voiced and voiceless, stopped and fricative: guirme, crìdh, chràdh, cluinn, chaoidh, cruaidh. Blue, heart, pain, hear, always, hard. Cruachan.

As best I can tell, DRAX and Drax the Destroyer and Drax Global and James Drax and Drax, West Yorkshire, are all of no relation. Except, perhaps, very deep: draco. The dragon who became the drake and the dragoon, the duck and the musket. From the Proto-Indo-European *derk-, to see.

In the anthology *Poems of the Scottish Hills*, the editor and mountaineer Hamish Brown apologises for his own reasoning for excluding centuries of Gaelic poetry. 'The hills form such a background to the Highland culture,' he says, 'that few poems actually are fully hill pieces.' The book is instead devoted to 'recreational mountain activities'.

Hillwalking makes a mountain poem, but living with a mountain does not.

Work and love and exile and protest are not suitable subjects for mountain poems.

Cruachan Beann is keening under deer, under sheep, under Gore-Tex.

Brown's own poem to Beinn Nibheis, the highest mountain in these islands, whose name means heavenly or poisonous or something wholly unknown, is called 'The Harlot'. 'I have come to hate that bitch,' he says.

From the ridge, looking down, I see trees in the gullies, on the slopes, across the landscape. From here, I cannot tell them apart. Is that a square of Sitka, harsh line against the hillside, shaped like great pinecones, planted dark and thick so that little else can grow? Is it a stand of new Scots pine, tall and tapering, brown to red, flourish of blue-green at the tops? Or one of the scraps of the old woods, windblown and wildformed?

In Canada, after clearing the people, Scots pine were planted to hold together the soil made vulnerable by taking down the Sitka for warships. In Scotland, after clearing the people to Canada, Sitka were planted to hold together the economy made vulnerable by the collapse of wool prices. Now, 43 per cent of Scotland's forest is Sitka and only 13 per cent Scots pine. Only 2 per cent of Scotland's woodland is older than a century; 56 per cent of Scotland's woodland is owned by absentee landlords. The numbers pile up. Looking out over the landscape, I can't see the percentages, but I can see the clear views.

Both Sitka and Scots pine are now called invasive in their new homes, and in some areas they do push out species not found anywhere else. The capercaillie does not stalk Sitka plantations, and is on its way to being made extinct in Scotland for the second time. But the history of plants, like the history of people, is a history of movement. And as the statement from Scottish Forestry says, it's not helpful to demonise one species of tree against another.

Beinn is a feminine word and càrn is masculine, cruach feminine and stob masculine.

For all it matters. Boireannach, woman, is a masculine word.

A tree can be the feminine craobh or the masculine crann. Craobh-ola is an olive tree. Crann-ola is an oil rig. A turbine is a wind tree, a pylon is a power tree.

Sometimes, when a man passes me on the hill, he says, 'Hi, hen.' Sometimes, he says, 'Hi, pal.' Sometimes, he says, 'Hi…'

From every damned step on the slopes, the dam.

In 2006, the first Camp for Climate Action took place at Drax power station in West Yorkshire. Hundreds of protestors, children among them, marched with ostrich puppets to the high fences. Two climbed a pylon on the perimeter, four broke into the station, and thirty-eight were arrested. The company's press statement claimed that we caused no disruption, but we knew otherwise. Over the next five years, we obstructed the runway at Heathrow, shut down Kingsnorth power station for a day, occupied the Bishopsgate in London, and broke into Royal Bank of Scotland headquarters in Edinburgh. Kingsnorth eventually fell, the third runway has not yet been built, and RBS divested from the Alberta tar sands – but Drax still stands.

For most of these years we were spied on by Mark Kennedy, a man whose name was Flash, a police spy licensed by the state to manipulate and rape. At Drax he was arrested twice for his performances, once for locking himself to a fence and once for assault. We will never truly know which protest plans we made ourselves and which the police made for us.

After I was beaten by police on the Bishopsgate, it took fifteen years before I could take part in such an occupation again, could put my body between the machinery of destruction and its operators. The fifteen years passed. I sat with a hundred others outside a glassy building on the outskirts of Edinburgh on a warm morning as the sky blued over the business park, blocking the entrance to an electronics factory that manufactures parts for weapons which are sold to perpetrate genocide in Gaza. For five hours I watched each movement of the police, unable to sing or speak. 'You can do this,' I told myself. 'You've done it before. You are doing it. You'll do it again.'

Round the clock of the ridge: the hill of the herd, the hill of fruit, the hill of horses, the dock-covered hill, the sling hill, the red stake, the grey bridge, the stag's stake, the chick's beak, the rough stake, the rutting peak.

Between them: the red corrie, the corrie of the crook, the corrie of the cloak, the snowy corrie, the cat's corrie, the sheep's corrie, the treeless rocky corrie, the grey corrie. In the heart of them all, the corrie of the peaks.

Names are for navigating and remembering, for telling you where to walk and where to gather, for reminding you what threats to watch out for and what treasures may be found. Now, the military technology of global positioning does the work instead, and the names become codes for the walker to decipher and mispronounce. Instead of following the landscape, I follow a satellite, my feet marking a little blue trail on my screen, thicker and more blue than a river.

The horses and cats are gone, but the sheep and deer still herd. The snow has melted, and all the corries are treeless. The fruit is gone and the docks remain. Still, sometimes, you will hear the rutting, but no one uses a sling any more except for pleasure. Whose crook? Whose cloak?

In the shadow of Cruachan Beann lived a woman whose name was Deirdre. When she was born, the chief druid foretold that she would be the most beautiful woman in Èirinn, and so beautiful that the country would go to war over her. King Conchobar kidnapped her and had her raised in a secret keep, but when she grew she fell in love with his most handsome warrior, Naoise. They fled across the water to Alba, and settled in Gleann Èite, beneath the peak of peaks. They lived happily there, until the king tricked them home, and what happened next gave Deirdre the name Sorrow.

*

Less often, I pass another woman on the mountain. Less often still another woman alone, a woman not walking in the warmth of other women, or walking – and why should this still be true? – behind a man.

When she greets me, sometimes there's ease and sometimes hesitation. Who am I speaking to? What does this person's body mean to me? Why should one body mean safety and the other danger? Why should this still be true?

We see what we expect to see. What our bodies remember.

As they walk through the Aldhani Highlands, a rebel explains to a thief the history of the planet. 'There used to be hundreds of settlements up here,' he says. 'Forty thousand Aldhanis all across the Highlands. They were here for centuries, but it only took the Empire a decade to clear them out. [...] Drove them south. There's an Enterprise Zone in the Lowlands. Factories, new towns, Imperial housing.'

In Alastair Mackenzie's 1883 *History of the Highland Clearances*, he quotes a Mr Somerville of Lochgilphead on the depopulation of the lands around Cruachan Beann. 'About nine miles of country on the west side of Loch Awe, in Argyllshire, that formerly maintained 45 families, are now rented by one person as a sheep farm [...]. The work of eviction commenced by giving, in many cases, to the ejected population, facilities and pecuniary aid for emigration; but now the people are turned adrift, penniless and shelterless, to seek a precarious subsistence on the sea-board, in the nearest hamlet or village, and in the cities, many of whom sink down helpless paupers on our poor-roll.'

'There's still a few shepherds in the hills,' says the rebel on Aldhani. 'Nature lovers, mystics, dead-enders.'

Television viewers. Poets. Hillwalkers.

Deirdre sings Gleann Èite:

Gleann measach iasgach linneach,
a thulcha corra is áille cruithneacht;
bheith dá iomrádh damhsa is deacrach,
gleann beachach na mbuabhall mbeannach.

(Fruitful, fishful, poolful glen / His round hillocks and lovely grains / To tell of him hurts me / Beeful glen of horned oxen)

She sings six more stanzas, naming thrush, fox, clover, deer, oak, raven, badger, hawk, blaeberry, otter, ivy and more, each in their relation to slope and water and woman. And it all hurts to sing.

One step to the next, the mirror of the corrie of the peaks winks to me. A photo flash in the corner of my eye, but when I turn my head it's dark and still. I rock back and forward on my feet. Forward, and the mirror shines white; backward, and the mirror is deep and black. Three steps forward, and the granite of the flanks does likewise, blinking white into waterfall and black into fissure. I put my head down and walk on.

*

Did anyone ever meet a mountain that they had not first heard in song or seen on a screen? Is there a difference between the two?

In 2021, a woman whose name was Warner blocked a freight train outside Drax power station in protest against forest-burning. During her trial the jury asked the judge for advice, saying that 'as a matter of conscience we are finding it difficult to come to a verdict'. The judge instructed them, 'You have all taken an oath or affirmation to try this case on the evidence, not your conscience.' Evidence convicted her. But in 1610, according to a plaque in the Old Bailey, two men were tried for preaching to an unlawful assembly, and the judge gave a verdict establishing 'The Right of Juries to give their Verdict according to their Convictions'.

In 2023, a woman whose name was Warner, another woman, another Warner of no relation, held a sign outside a trial of environmental protestors which read: 'Jurors you have an absolute right to acquit a defendant according to your conscience'. She was arrested for contempt of court, and defendants were likewise punished for speaking about their reasons for protesting at their trials. The campaign group Defend Our Juries fought the arrest, by organising mass demonstrations of people holding up the same signs until it became impossible for the state to prosecute. In 2024, Warner's charges were dismissed.

In 2025, the UK government proscribed the protest organisation Palestine Action, who for years had taken direct action against the arms manufacturers and military bases implicated in the occupation of and genocide in Gaza. It became illegal under the Terrorism Act to organise as Palestine Action or to support them in any way. At a meeting in the week of the proscription, I listened to Huda Ammori, co-founder of Palestine Action, speak of the life-giving work of physically obsctructing genocide, and then I listened to Tim Crosland, co-founder of Defend Our Juries, the first person ever to be found in contempt of the Supreme Court for his civil disobedience over attempts to build a third runway at Heathrow, outline a plan: every week, people would gather with placards supporting Palestine Action, and each week there would be more of them until they became impossible to arrest, the same strategy that had defended jurors' consciences. As I write, the numbers are growing, and so are the arrests. And the genocide continues.

The rebels' hike in Aldhani begins in Gleann Teilt, up above Blàr Athall, on the edge of the Monadh Ruadh, the red mountains, which in English, named for only one of many peaks, becomes the Cairngorms, blue and ungrammatically plural. Language shift flips from one end of the spectrum to the other. As on Aldhani, the slopes are only green and grey. The wind and the clouds are the same on both planets.

In Scotland, it's a thirty-hour hike from Gleann Teilt to the Cruachan Dam, longer if you need to keep to the slopes and passes to avoid imperial settlements. West along Loch Teimheil, south through Mòr-choille Tatha, and then along pretty Gleann Lìomhann. You'd pass the yew at Fartairchill, the oldest living thing in these islands, who remembers once living in an old-growth forest of Scots pine. Then it's over another pass and through Gleann Urchaidh, with as little time as possible spent on the A roads, packed with logging trucks and drivers making their way to their chosen Munro. The rebels manage this hike in only a night of walking, and when they arrive at the Cruachan Dam, the Imperial base, the actor on the screen, the power station I can see from each summit, stood beneath it is an outsize fibreglass model of the Queen's Well in Gleann Marc, 150 miles back east. Time and space collapse on television, and everyone, everywhere, plays a role.

I reach the last summit, Stob Dàimh. Once, someone at the military technology of Ordnance Survey mistranscribed the peak: it became Diamh, and stayed Diamh in a hundred walking guides. Always, at the summit, I think with relief: it's all downhill from here.

I can't be at a summit without thinking of a painting: Caspar David Friedrich's *Der Wanderer über dem Nebelmeer*, the lone, overcoated man surveying an impossible collection of rocky peaks, each sampled from a different part of the Elbsandsteingebirge. He is conquest and the lonely sublime. I know the nonsense of the story, but what sort of woman doesn't also love being on top of the world? Of course I've come here to see what I can achieve. Of course I've come here to feel alone with the mountains, above the corries and glens which once were busy with work and love and protest and praise. As I watch the horizon, another hiker speeds past on his sticks.

A few hills to the south and west, in the lands where Somerville spoke of the evicted people, I see a white wind farm. It belongs to Beinn Ghlas, the grey hill. Nestled among the turbines' trunks, I know, is a dry-stone wall, a bell and a statue: *A Shieling for Deirdre and Naoise.* The estate owner, Sam Macdonald, had the artwork built as a memorial for his wife. Who can begrudge anyone for telling a story where they need it? The lovers' stone statue was gilded by a woman whose name is Gray.

The wind farm was built by Ventient Energy, which in 2024 merged with Renantis to form Nadara, which is the Gaelic word for 'natural' misspelled so as not to confuse the Anglophone tongue. Nadara's website claims that they are one of the largest renewable independent power producers in Europe, and that my visit to their website to learn this generated 0.04g of carbon dioxide.

In *The Second Olive Tree*, the Palestinian poet Mahmoud Darwish praises the olive tree, tree of peace and abundance, in the wake of Israel's decades-long destruction of the groves. The state has felled over a million trees in the past forty years. Darwish names the tree a grandmother, describes her roots in the sky. In protest, a boy throws a stone and is killed. In the poem, his body will grow the next tree. 'And,' Darwish says at the end, in Marilyn

Hacker's English translation (Darwish's Arabic beyond what I in my limits can source or quote), 'green!'

In the episode of *Andor* entitled 'The Axe Forgets', a rebel tells a thief about his brother, a pepper tree farmer. 'Imperial Prefect came in, took his land, flooded it,' he says. 'He couldn't fight him. He couldn't bear it, so he went out on a boat and filled his pockets with stones.' His eyes are bright when he talks about the trees. 'Centuries of 'em,' he says. In a later episode, a worker uses a stone as a weapon against Imperial police, who open fire. The stone contains the ashes of a rebel.

As a strategy of colonisation, Israel has planted thousands of acres of trees across the desert, often over Palestinian settlements the state has destroyed. In 2025, in one of these plantations, Eshtaol Forest, pines caught fire. Wildfires spread faster through monoculture. Within a week, thousands of acres had burned.

In 2025, Scotland saw more wildfires than in any other recorded year. On scrub kept low and dry by deer and grouse-shooting, by mountain recreation, the last scraps of a Highland economy, thousands of acres burned.

Did anyone ever join a rebellion who had not first heard a story about how to resist? Which stories can you trust?

Below the last summit is a little black pool set into the heath, shrinking in the sun, and in the little pool are twenty dead frogs. Their white bellies turn up against the sky. Their thin brown limbs are frozen in the mud, like abandoned plastic toys. I stand next to a tall, thin man. Do I recognise him from a peak? Do I recognise his voice?

'What happened?' he asks. But I don't know. 'The heat?' I wonder. 'Maybe,' he says. 'But there's still plenty spawn in there.' 'Would this be normal?' Neither of us know the life cycle of mountain frogs. Neither of us knows what is normal. We stand next to each other, staring. The frogs lie still. The sun burns. I leave the bodies behind.

One of the rebels on Aldhani is a young poet called Nemik. He writes poetry and manifestos about the glory of the revolution. During the heist he is crushed beneath a sliding heap of gold.

In his manifesto, he says, in a text distributed around the galaxy by Cassian Andor, and around the Earth by the Walt Disney Corporation, the second biggest media company in the world, which donated $2 million in aid to Israel in October 2023, which is a priority target for consumer boycotts by the Palestinian-led Boycott, Divestment and Sanctions Movement for its role in employing cultural ambassadors for Israel and for promoting stories of Israel's colonial project, 'the Imperial need for control is so desperate because it is so unnatural. Tyranny requires constant effort. It breaks, it leaks.'

Always, as I'm leaving a mountain, I say out loud: 'Tapadh leibh.' Thank you, you with respect, you in the plural. I offer my gratitude to something that is always more than itself.

*

Aldhani isn't the Gàidhealtachd. The Gàidhealtachd isn't Palestine. A Sitka spruce isn't a Scots pine. A plantation isn't a forest. A hill isn't a lover. A walk isn't a life. A man isn't a woman. A poem isn't a protest. A reservoir isn't a lochan. A power station isn't a shieling. A mountain isn't a wilderness. A story isn't a truth. A càrn isn't a cruach. A summit isn't an end.

I'm lurching down from Stob Garbh, the rough stab, along the flank of Beinn a' Bhùiridh, the roaring hill. The dam rises and lengthens, greeting my return. I don't know how I can make it through this last hour, even with gravity's aid. Back over the gantry, through the birches, past the granny oak. There's hardly strength in my limbs, but less choice. I have to finish the round. Back to my little red car, a hothouse on this out-of-season day. Back along Lòchadh and Faolan and Dochart and Ògal, a darkness and a saint and waters old enough that their names have no meaning beyond their sound. Back down the road, spitting exhaust behind me. Back home.

A Partial History of Walking with Pain

Polly Atkin

It is a bright May morning in 2007. I am paused, partway up the rocky staircase that forms the first section of the path up the side of Stickle Ghyll from Old Dungeon Ghyll, in the Langdale Valley of the Lake District. I have ostensibly stopped to take a photograph, but really I have stopped because I need to. I have been trying to keep up with my companions, but with each metre it is getting harder.

My heart is beating too fast and I can't catch my breath. My mouth is dry from panting and my back is uncomfortably damp. I look up and feel a wave of dizziness and nausea. There is a cold wind coming down from the tops, chilling my fingers and nose, but I have had to shed all my layers from the effort of ascent.

I look down, back, turning slowly, steadying myself against the sudden feeling I could just tumble all the way into the green valley we rose from. The river glints as it winds away eastwards. In the distance, the shimmer of a lake. Layers of hazy blue mountains blurring into hazy blue sky. We have come so far already.

I am with a group from the university I am studying at. They are all scholars of Romantic literature, steeped in the landscape and literature of the Lakes. To walk in it is part of a scholarly practice. We are walking to learn more about the place and the people we are studying, more about the way they knew place. We are learning through our bodies, but I do not realise that I am learning a different history – a history of my own body, a history of undiagnosed illness, a history of disability: my own, and others.

My PhD supervisor, metres ahead of me, pauses in his easy exertion, and turns to me with concern.

I am remembering how much I hate walking in a group like this, walking to the pace of others, others who seem to be able to keep moving and moving with no apparent consequence, as though their bodies are balloons they have let float uphill at no cost to themselves. How much I hate lagging behind, feeling like I am pulling them backwards with my slowness. How do they do it? Each step feels like I am pushing the whole globe up this small mountain, and all its gravity is pushing back down through my every bone, every joint.

I thought I was prepared for this. I've been walking every day, walking to campus along the back lanes, walking for miles along the greening canal towpaths and footpaths surrounding the village where I've been living.

But I had forgotten what it means to push yourself upwards, not along. How much more it takes. I wanted to be here. I want to be here. But I wasn't prepared for how much pain would be here with me. I thought I could get away from it. That if I just kept going, I could leave it behind.

I refuse to turn. I refuse to give up. I refuse to go down.

Because when we drew into the car park, I realised I'd been here before, almost ten years previously.

I hadn't remembered the name, but as soon as I saw it, I knew it. The scene of my great failure. The scene of my humiliation and defeat. The day I returned to the school minibus sobbing, the walk leader carrying my pack. The day I became an irrevocable liability.

The day that gave the lie to my delusion of recovery, from which my life splintered and took its own different path.

When I am walking, I am walking with pain. If I am walking, I am in pain. This is how it is to walk in my body. I walk with and in pain wherever I am walking. No matter the map, no matter the geography, my immediate location is pain. No matter the company, I am accompanied by pain. Pain my companion. Unshakeable. Pain my shadow. Pain my guide. Pain always there for me, especially when I don't seek it. Pain my destination. I know this now. I know it as plain fact. No drama. But back then I thought I could outwalk it. That if I slipped behind a rock and hid, it would pass me by and I could continue on without it. That it was something outside me and not part of me. That I could slough it off, or have it removed with a small procedure. That it was not me, not mine, not for me.

*

It is an overcast day in June 1998. I am paused partway up the rocky staircase that forms the first section of the path up the side of Stickle Ghyll from Old Dungeon Ghyll, in the Langdale Valley of the Lake District, although I will not remember these names. I have ostensibly stopped to adjust my pack, but really I have stopped because I need to. I have been trying to keep up with my companions, but with each metre it is getting harder.

I am in so much pain. My heart is beating too fast and I can't catch my breath. Every time I lift my leg to pull myself up another step, a pain like molten metal shoots through my left hip, and the more I try to shift weight away from it, the more my right knee complains. Two of my toenails are falling off after yesterday's walk up the Old Man of Coniston, and I feel them scrape against the top of my boots, rubbing looser, looser, agitating the bruised skin underneath. I'm not sure how much further I can go. With each metre I am getting slower, closer to seizing up entirely.

I am with a group from school. We are training for an expedition to Madagascar that we have been planning for all year. It is meant to be a celebration of leaving school, something to prepare us for the world to come, something to be proud of.

This weekend we are walking six miles each day carrying full packs to prepare for it. This is our second training weekend. Our first was in March, in Devon, and I managed that. I slept in a tent with ice forming on the outside, and crossed an icy river at dawn. I worked with my teammates to put up and take down and carry our tent, and all on a diet of kidney beans and white rice because the group who had been assigned to buy supplies had forgotten my dietary requirements. I'd done all that, and no one who didn't know me well would have known that I was still seeing doctors for inexplicable fatigue that had felled me the year before. That just a few days after I was wading across that river I would be discharged from a clinic, with the assessment: 'Miss Atkin seems to be improving, although I cannot say why.'

I have been practising carrying a pack at home, but it's been hard, fitting in walks between exams and rest. This is a test. I am trying to prove to myself and everyone else that I am better. I couldn't have done this last year. I couldn't have even got the pack on my back. That much I should be proud of, shouldn't I?

Our leader, Adrian, ex-SAS, does not believe in pain. He has made this very clear. To show pain is to let yourself down and to let your team down. If I lean forward I can still see the car park. I am letting the team down already and we have barely begun.

I will not let him see me weaken. I stifle my sobs, grit my teeth, and keep climbing.

My history of walking is a history of accumulating pain. When I first walked, I walked with my toes turned in so far I tripped over them. I stumbled and fell, but I carried on walking, running, dancing. I was everywhere, limbs flung in all directions. If there was pain, the pain was so usual it did not stop me. I do not remember the pain.

When I was eighteen months old, I broke my leg, and though I know there was plenty of pain, I also know that once my leg was safely encased in plaster I carried on walking, running, dancing, leaping. I could not be stopped. I ran the foot of the plaster bare again and again.

When I was four I broke the other leg. I remember the pain of that one, the memory of pain. Once the plaster was on, I kept moving. Afterwards, my leg was weak, and it was harder to move, but hadn't it always been hard? Hadn't my feet always bent strangely, my ankles collapsed, my hips clicked painfully? Didn't I always keep walking and running and dancing anyway?

There were times I couldn't, of course. Times I was sick as well as in pain, and we brought out the old pushchair, and I let myself be driven around in it like a toddler or a princess, so that I could still go on an outing I would have missed otherwise. These things were mere facts of our lives. I was in pain, or sickly, most of the time, and I could not walk, so we found other ways.

I was in and out of outpatients all the time but no one could offer any real advice or help. In desperation, my mum took me to see a private consultant, and he told her to keep me moving, keep me walking, keep me dancing, that moving will help.

The next time I have a plaster cast on my leg it is for broken ligaments, not a bone, and this time the pain follows me once the plaster is cut off, will not be shed.

My knees have been growing more and more painful and I have been told to give up dance classes, give up swimming. After the plaster cast comes off, I sheathe the extraordinary rainbow colours of my bruised leg in a Tubigrip to support it, but it hurts all day and is hard to move. One day I trip in the classroom, my foot snagged on the carpet tiles, and fall. The agony is so sharp and sudden I can't stop the tears, and the tears are so total and consuming my friends laugh at me. My pain is a kind of ugly crying that is not acceptable. They do not believe in the pain, and that is another kind of pain. I learn it is better to try and swallow the pain, to let it implode, not explode, if I can.

With each year that passes there is another injury, something new that makes walking harder. A dislocated knee. A fall. Another fall. Time passing is an accumulation of pain.

I keep walking, though I don't run any more.

The pain likes to appear in unexpected places. My stomach. Urinary tract. My tonsils. When I am fifteen I begin to experience strange dizzy spells, a feeling that I am falling out of time, no longer connected to the ground. It is very tiring to feel like this, and it is not surprising that soon I am feeling increasingly listless, increasingly exhausted. I am finding it hard to keep moving at all.

I dislocate my knee again. I break my elbow.

I get worse. There are many tests. My B12 is low. My red blood cells are malformed. My white blood cell count is alarming. There are more tests but none are conclusive. I get worse and worse. I do not fit any known disease profile. Phrases like post-viral fatigue are used interchangeably with ME and chronic fatigue syndrome. There is no treatment for any of these, but I am sent to psychology, with the hope they will help me.

Psychology is so terrible we seek refuge in alternative medicine. Reflexology, specialised diets. They help a bit.

School wants me to take a year off to get better, but I'm not sure I will get better if no one can say what is wrong with me, so I refuse. I do not want to fall behind. I do not want to be left behind.

I keep going. The pain and the fatigue live in me and I have learnt how to move without disturbing them, how to keep them a little steady inside me. Together like this we get a little stronger.

And so I find myself halfway up to Stickle Tarn, realising with horror that I have miscalculated the weight of the pain, that I have disturbed it after all, and that I cannot carry it by myself.

In my diary the following Tuesday I write: 'But nonetheless the view was simply spectacular, the scenery unbelievably beautiful. Only marred by the pain, just ever so slightly.'

In 2007 we have been reading Dorothy Wordsworth's record of her ascent of Scafell in October 1818. It is famous now as the first first-hand account of mountaineering by a woman, and the first recorded ascent of England's highest peak by a woman, although for years many readers assumed the writer was Dorothy's brother, William. The account was first published within William's 1822 *Guide to the Lakes* as 'an extract from a letter to a Friend'. In the 1823 edition of the guide he included Dorothy's tour of Ullswater too, similarly uncredited, at her request. It makes sense that people would assume the walker, the writer, was William himself.

Dorothy is forty-six at the time of this climb, Mary Barker, her companion, forty-four. They have a guide, John Allison, a porter to carry their things, and Barker's maid Agnes with them, so there are actually three women on the expedition, though I don't remember us talking about that back then. Mary Barker is an artist. In the letter, Dorothy describes her as 'an active climber of the hills' – a woman with 'resources within herself'.[1] They are going with a painter's mission, to seek a 'magnificent prospect', not for the sake of walking in and of itself. The first part of the journey is taken in a cart, then they go by foot up to Esk Hause (which Dorothy called 'Ash Course'), where they are rewarded with their first magnificent views – of 'peculiar deliciousness'.

They look down on the Langdale Pikes, and the long narrow valley of Langdale.

But they also look up at Scafell Pike. The summit seems so close they are called on by it. It is further than they think, of course, but they make it, and eat their dinner on the summit in the sun, watching a storm roll in. Dorothy writes of seeing 'mighty masses of cloud which came boiling over the mountains. Great Gavel, Helvellyn, and Skiddaw were wrapped in storm; yet Langdale, and the mountains in that quarter were all bright with sunshine.'

The rain reaches them, then the Langdales, which are soon 'decorated by two splendid rainbows'. The rainbows connect them to friends on their own walk – William Wilberforce and his family, and Sir George and Lady Beaumont, who have taken the slightly gentler journey that day up Skiddaw. Watching the rainbows move over Skiddaw, they think of the Wilberforces, their thoughts and their friends brought together by the intermingling of light and water.

I can't remember if we spoke of any of this on that trip in 2007. I remember we talked about the obvious things. The challenge the women set themselves. The important record the letter became. The history of women walking, and the history of the Lake District as a history of walking. The literature of the Lake District as a literature of walking.

This is how I thought of it then, and for many years after. I had no sense of a literature of the Lakes that was not a literature of walking, in some way or other, whether climbing peaks or walking for work. I had no sense of what a way of knowing the Lakes that was not through walking might be.

I was about to move from just outside Lancaster to Grasmere, to begin my field research for my PhD, which centred on perceptions of the Lake District and, more widely, on how places become the places they are. How they gather meanings.

No one would have known that day on that walk that before I had left London the previous year I had been in such pain again that I had been struggling to walk from my house to the tube station. That I had been terrified I was getting very ill again, and that this time I might not get better.

Yet here I am, halfway up a mountain. Halfway up a mountain and realising that mountain was the museum of so much pain.

But dear lord, the view is delicious, isn't it? The most vivid and exquisite beauty.

In 1998, I do not record my humiliation in detail. It is a particular kind of pain. There is no attention to the wise or funny words of my companions, no keen eye on the 'never-dying lichens' or cushions of moss that Dorothy Wordsworth was able to describe. My account is spare and full of gaps.

I write how I was '100m from the top of the first "hill", climbing near vertical rocks' when I broke down. I was holding everyone back, and they couldn't wait any more. I was so slow, I was in danger of ruining the whole trip. I couldn't catch up with them. I couldn't keep moving. The pain came out of me as a flow of tears so heavy I couldn't breathe through them. Our ex-SAS leader, palpably disgusted, took my pack. It was clear this was a form of humiliation in itself. I had been found wanting. I had failed the test.

I remember this only in flashes – blurs of grey slate and green grass – the memory of pain as a concept, not a felt thing. More than anything, the memory of my sick horror as I realised the extent of my failure.

Even without the pack, I was struggling, shaking. My hip and now my knee too, and my bruised and throbbing toes, and the pain itself so disconcerting, even without the exertion of crying, of admitting defeat, which brought its own particular unsteadiness.

It is no surprise that I stumbled and fell in the beck. That when I fell, I hit the elbow I had broken the autumn before on a smooth, Lake District stone. That in that fragile state, body stiff with carrying the pain, I thought I had broken my elbow again. That I could not straighten my arm, and thought I had destroyed the entire summer with my body's carelessness.

That I finished the walk relieved it had started raining, because I could tell myself it concealed the tears I could not stop leaking out of my eyes, even though I was keeping them quiet this time.

I remember feeling every cell of my body shaking with the effort of keeping walking.

Then back at school, I was told plainly what I knew the moment I handed over my pack. I was a liability. I was not strong enough for Madagascar. I would let everyone down with my catastrophic weakness. I had to agree it was best I did not go. No good would come of it for anyone.

That was what the Lake District meant to me then. My failure made manifest in two bruised toenails which fell off, one by one, that summer, turning eighteen with the nubs of their successors pushing them out of position.

And then I forgot about the Lake District.

I remembered my humiliation. I remembered lost Madagascar. I remembered being made to accept my limits against my will. I did not remember the place where it happened.

I remember too, though, how I trained for that expedition by sending my vast existential restlessness and teenage dissatisfaction out of the house on long, unplanned walks, following local footpaths out from my suburban home on the fringes of Nottingham into the surrounding countryside. Along embankments of disused railways, through fields and woods usually hidden to view behind the interlacing channels of the ring road. How walking became a way of thinking, became a way of processing. Walking as cognition. Walking as rewriting.

How, despite the fatigue and pain always dragging at me, there was something in the motion of walking that felt not good so much as necessary, regardless of the discomfort I trod through. That need to move, to be always moving.

How I wrote poems as I walked, sang songs, memorised lines from books. How I thought and unthought and rethought, unspooling the tangles of my thinking and stretching them out as I went. Un-labyrinthing them.

All the years I lived in London when I would walk across the city to avoid paying a tube fare, but also because I needed to keep moving. The discomfort beneath it. Walking with pain because walking was moving my mind along with my body, and easing a different kind of pain.

How I knew my dad felt this way about walking. That walking was a way for him of extending his own great restlessness into endless space. My dad is a person who prefers to be on the move. He likes moving dwellings: boats, caravans. He loves the road, he loves to be in transit. He is happiest like this.

He had discovered walking for pleasure in his late thirties, when he started to go on long walks with his uncle Jack. All my childhood I thought of him as a walker. In those years, he said, he thought he could walk forever once he was set going, like a self-winding watch. He would just keep walking.

But in his late fifties he became a companion of pain. His feet swelled. To put weight on them was excruciating. He was struggling to move around at work. He suddenly did not know any more how to keep moving.

He was researching the best options for wheelchairs when tests revealed it was psoriatic arthritis affecting his feet. It took a few years of trying out different options, but eventually he found a medication that worked enough to keep the pain bounded, allowed him to keep walking, even if not the same kind of distances as before.

This is what I think of when I think of walking – the balance of pain and the need to keep moving – when I try to understand why I keep going, why I keep moving with the pain.

I think of how lucky I am, to have lived a life in which I can choose to walk for my enjoyment, rather than necessity. Of the extraordinary privilege of that.

I don't walk far these days, and I don't walk high, but to walk itself is a kind of self-soothing, even as it hurts. Everything hurts. Sitting hurts too. So why not walk? A little bit of walking, just to keep the yawning abyss of restlessness at bay, just enough to feel like I'm in motion.

I think about this often, on my tiny, very local walks, how good it feels to turn my legs like cogs locking into the world.

In 2007 I took my pauses for breath, and I carried on. At Stickle Tarn we stopped for lunch, shared tea and read – maybe poetry – maybe Dorothy. I don't remember. Some of us carried on up to the pike, some stayed lower. I wanted to reach what I had missed before. Taking time, it was possible. We sat on the summit and looked out at the ripples of fells below us until they melted into haze. We talked and took our time. Watched boats moving on Windermere in the distance. We wore sunglasses and fleeces in the May sun. I felt a sense of triumph and sadness I could not begin to articulate. I have a photo of me at the summit. I look calm and happy. I am holding a biscuit in one hand. It was a good day in good company. The kind of company who will wait for you if you need them to, and will not evaluate you a failure for it.

We had a drink at the Old Dungeon Ghyll pub and went back to our hostel, delighted with our collective achievement.

Dorothy described her and Mary's walk up Scafell as an 'uncommon performance'.

There was nothing particularly special to anyone else about our walk that day, but to me it meant a world of possibility unrolling at my feet like those green fells and distant lakes. A life I had thought impossible. It was the first time I had walked up a mountain since the last time I had walked up that same mountain and felt I had failed at everything.

I thought wrong things about it in 2007 too. I thought that reaching the top meant I was better, or betterish, at last. That I had left the sick version of myself behind, sunk her in the bog. Even when my knees swelled up like bruised persimmons in the days that followed.

I thought I had come full circle and been granted some kind of reprieve. Days later I would move into an attic room in Grasmere and begin a summer of exploring the surrounding fells with new friends, spending the long light summer evenings high above the valleys.

I didn't know I was in a pause of unusual wellness that would last only a year or so before it started to wane. I didn't know there were other ways of knowing this place that were just as delicious, just as splendid.

I had to get very ill again, very in the pain again, before I learnt this. Before I learnt that, in thinking only of summitting, I had missed so many other ways of knowing the Lake District. I had missed so much other art and literature of the Lake District, too. Most importantly, I had missed myself.

In 1818, Dorothy Wordsworth is entering a period of unusual wellness that lasted around a decade. During these years she walks more for pleasure perhaps than at any other time in her life, both in the Lakes and on trips away. The young poet Maria Jane Jewsbury writes of her extraordinary blend of 'green vigour with grey maturity' in these years.[2] But she would not repeat her walk up Scafell any more than I would repeat my walk up Langdale Pike.

Dorothy Wordsworth has long been praised for her 'extraordinary physical strength' as well as her sensitivity and creative receptivity – praised for being a person of 'buoyant frame and fervid spirit' in the words of John Campbell Shairp.[3] This vision of Dorothy as exceptionally physically and mentally powerful has persisted from the nineteenth century through the twentieth, and continues to dominate impressions of her. It is the one I was introduced to, the one I knew in 2007.

Dorothy has been held up as a symbol of women's strength. She is the epitome of the walking woman, the godmother of walking literature. This is how she is described, in book after book after book.

I had known little about her before I started my PhD, and I absorbed uncritically the notion of her as physically robust and physically fit, even as I read again and again her Grasmere journals, with their endless litany of headaches and bowel aches and toothaches, and days spent unwell in bed. Did I not tally the two? Or did I not want to see what became obvious to me, that the two things can co-exist in the same person, the same body, as most chronically ill people know? One week we can walk and find great joy in it. Another we cannot leave our bed.

In March 1829, aged fifty-seven, Dorothy became gravely ill while staying with her nephew John in Leicestershire. In May she wrote to her dear friend Henry Crabb Robinson, 'it is the first time in my life of fifty-six years in which I have had a serious illness' (DW to HCR, 2 May 1829).[4] This was the beginning of five years of intermittent near-fatal health crises, each of which left her with additional impairments, and made walking harder and harder.

Once returned to her home in Rydal in May 1829, she seemed to everyone to be 'healthy and well', but found herself getting unusually tired after walking only a mile or two. To Samuel Taylor Coleridge, who always wrote and spoke openly to Dorothy of his own digestive problems, she described the 'serious derangements of the Bowels' that had troubled her ever since March 1829 (DW to STC, 14 November 1829). To her close friend Catherine Clarkson, Dorothy described how 'sickness and violent perspirations – hot and cold', and daily, constant pains in her bowels were also affecting her legs and her ability to stand and move (DW to CC, 18–27 October 1829). These attacks kept recurring, and each successive episode left Dorothy weaker and less able to support her own weight. The family borrowed a Merlin chair – a kind of proto-wheelchair – which she used to move around the garden terraces. Later she was pulled around in a small carriage similar to a bath chair. In these years she walked in mind and memory, not in place, but found great solace and freedom in those imaginative walks.

Most scholars and biographers have chosen to see the later part of Dorothy's life – the part in which she cannot walk long distances – as entirely separate to the part of her life in which she did. Almost as though she is two people: Walking Dorothy and Disabled Dorothy. In different ways by different people, Dorothy has been blamed for causing her own illness, whether by walking too much, working too much, being too sensitive, or not fulfilling her perceived potential as either a woman or a writer. She should have married, or she should have had her own literary career. She should have worked less, expected less. Walking Dorothy is held up for praise, Disabled Dorothy as a warning. Don't walk so much. Don't feel so much. Don't insist so much on taking your own path. People do not want to see continuity between these parts of her life, unless one is causing the other.

When I began to look into her own records of her life, I found a history both more complicated and more simple. Although 1829 marks the beginning of her serious illness, she was never exactly well. Even at her most well, she knew what it was like to live with pain, and with the shadow of pain. She carried the weight of pain when she walked all those miles.

In her letters and her journals, there is a long pattern of illness going back at least to Dorothy's late teens. A few weeks before her twentieth birthday, she writes to her best friend Jane Pollard that she has been ailing all year 'without being absolutely ill'. She reports having 'an extreme Weariness in my limbs after the most trifling Exertions such as going up stairs' and has been 'more troubled with Headache' (DW to Jane Pollard, 7 December 1791).

She recorded episodes of serious bowel problems throughout her life, which interrupt both her daily life and her walking. In 1801 William writes to their brother Richard that they have both been well, except 'Dorothy being subject to bilious sickness from time to time', which suggests her regular stomach upsets were simply a part of her life even then (WW to RW, 21 November 1801). Often these bowel problems are accompanied by problems walking, with pain and weakness in her legs, just as she describes in 1829. A long walk in 1808 is interrupted by a flare-up which leaves her desperately sick and wishing for home, followed by bowel problems the next day. She has to be taken home in a borrowed chaise. During a family tour of Europe in 1820, bowel symptoms limit her travel and sightseeing, often restricting her to her room. She writes to Catherine Clarkson, 'my legs ached so much from the state of my Bowels that I was forced upon the bed again' (DW to CC, 23 July 1820). She keeps a health log in 1820–1 detailing pain and 'disorde[r] in Bowels'.[5]

The poster-girl for walking in the Lake District was chronically ill all along. I had made the same mistake that others before me had, of assuming that a woman who walked was not also a woman who was ill, that walking and illness are mutually exclusive. I had separated Walking Dorothy and Disabled Dorothy in my mind, filing them away as separate entities without questioning the evidence or lack of it.

Through the years in which the distance I could walk shrank as Dorothy's had, I learnt the lie of this separation, both through my own body, and through Dorothy's body of work. Troubled by the way her illness was depicted, I went back to the source material and met a different Dorothy. A person of great strength of character and body but who lived her adult life with chronic pain of various kinds. A person to whom family was everything, but who never showed any desire to marry or have children of her own. A person who spent many years of her life housebound and in terrible agony, but who found her poetic voice in those years.

In the midst of her illness in the 1830s, Dorothy writes a series of poems she calls her 'sickbed consolations'. These poems reflect her hopes for the future, for recovery, but more than anything, they show her attempts to work out how to live with her new reality. The poems are a solace and a comfort in themselves, but also reach towards pleasure, joy, mitigation of grief and pain. They return to ideas and places from her brother's poems, and from their shared walks in their youth, but expand and rework them to reflect on her confinement. In the poems, the sickroom she has feared as a prison becomes a portal from which she can travel anywhere, through poetry, and through imagination. She writes of herself as walking – not with her body, but with her mind – far beyond the reaches of the map. She walks across memory, through time, through counties and countries. She has remade walking from her sickroom, and walked further than ever before without leaving her bed.

I wish I had known this Dorothy in 2009 when I became more ill again, or my symptoms became less displaceable. I had to find her myself, a long journey back to a disability history that was always there, but hidden beneath a veneer of healthfulness.

When I found this Dorothy, I began to realise that my history was always part of Lake District history. That not being able to walk was as much a part of being here as being able to walk. That neither one had more value than the other. I learnt from Dorothy that a garden made in a sickroom has as much imaginative power as one growing wild, and that walking in the mind can take you further than walking on a fell. I learnt that all of these things can co-exist at once. That a person can be in pain, and walk. That a person can walk, and walk with pain. That a person in pain can not walk, and still move. That walking does not have to mean moving. That moving, like bodies, is much more complicated and marvellous than we assume.

I still choose to walk. I walk with pain. Pain is my immediate location. Pain is my old familiar, reliable in its variousness. Sometimes I walk with one pain to avoid another. I accept the pain of the damaged nerve in my left foot to ease the pain of my slow digestion. I accept the pain of my clicking ankle to avoid the pain of a dislocating knee. I accept the pain of my slipping hip to avoid the eternal restlessness of the soul. It is a balance, as all things are.

I have learnt to live better with the pain. I have adjusted the way I live, the way I move, the things I expect of myself and the time I expect them to take. I have learnt not to try to keep pace with others, especially the kind of others who would leave you behind, who would judge you badly for slowness. I have learnt not to expect any of this to change, or not to change. That symptoms are shifting all the time, and that bodies change. That what a body needs will change too.

For now, I walk small. I walk local. I walk a repeating loop that includes parts of Dorothy's favourite repeating loop. I walk for light and I walk for the companionship of nature. I walk for the love of place and I walk for the love of movement. I walk with pain and I accept that pain as part of me, part of my complicated human life. I record the pain, because it matters that it was here. Because it is part of me. Without it, I would be a different iteration of me.

I have learnt to ask for help with the pain, and not to be afraid to cry. I have learnt that weakness is not a moral failing. I have learnt that sensitivity is not a result of poor character.

I am lucky to have painkillers that work and help keep me moving. I am lucky to have been able to adjust my life to put at its centre the need to keep moving. The world is full of peculiar deliciousness and I will find it where it finds me. Where I can be. While I can. I keep moving. I am lucky to have filled my life with people who will wait for me, keep pace with me, sit with me, rest with me. Value me as I am, as we all hope to be. As we all should be.

The Near Ways

Gail Simmons

Whenever I visit my mother in the Chilterns village where she has lived for almost sixty years, and where I grew up, the first thing I do – after dropping off my suitcase and sharing a cup of tea and a chat – is pull on the walking boots I keep there and head out to the bridleway that crosses the lane a hundred metres from the house. I don't need a map. This is a route I've walked for decades, and it's one I know as intimately as my mother's face.

The boots are an old pair, their soles worn flat from years of walking and their laces frayed, but their only sorties are on the gentle footpaths that lattice the hills and valleys around Ashley Green. My main pair are at home in North Yorkshire, and are in better nick. These are the ones I use for the longer-distance hikes I undertake as a travel writer specialising in walking. Their last serious outing was on the Old Way – the rediscovered pilgrimage route running some 230 miles from Southampton to Canterbury. I've also walked long-distance trails in Jordan and Syria wearing previous incarnations of these boots, and before that led groups through the hills of Tuscany, Umbria and Lazio, following ancient Etruscan roads, or treading in the footsteps of St Francis of Assisi. My first long-distance trail, however, was the Cotswold Way, which I walked after finishing university and wearing my first pair of proper walking boots, a long summer of freedom unravelling before me. I don't remember the boots, but each sun-gold day of that walk is engraved in my memory.

But my walking history did not begin on an official long-distance path. It began in the beech woods and flinty fields of the Chilterns chalklands, around the home where I grew up all those decades ago.

Here in Ashley Green, my old, worn boots are good enough for the walk I'm about to do. Old they may be, but there's something immensely reassuring about putting on footwear that has seen me through many hundreds of blister-free miles, and which I can't bear to throw out now that they're past their best. Moulded to the shape of my feet, they're as comforting to me as returning to my childhood home.

Turning right out of the drive, I follow the lane to the bridleway, its entrance a dark tunnel of trees. It's now signed Chiltern Heritage Trail. Long before it was given that name, and before the Victorian village church was built, this was the coffin route from Ashley Green to the parish church in Chesham. Today, in the age of the car and the crematorium, it's a leisure path shared by walkers and horse riders.

Stepping from the sunshine of the lane onto the bridleway is like plunging into a deep green ocean, the trees closing overhead like waves. Underfoot lies last year's leaf litter, layered over rich brown earth and imprinted with the hooves of horses and boots of walkers. Sunlight sifts through the canopy, the wind trembles the branches. Above the trees the sun is hot, but the air underneath is cool and damp. Birdsong draws me further into the tunnel, pulling me deeper into the village's rural past.

Bridleways are one of four designated public rights of way in Britain, along with footpaths and two types of byway. This one accounts for just two of the seventeen miles of rights of way enclosed within the parish of Ashley Green, and only a fragment of the estimated 150,000 miles that remain across Britain today. Established over centuries, most footpaths and bridleways evolved as links: between villages, connecting them to markets, towns and churches, and within them, tethering outlying fields, hamlets and farms. A millennium of steady use led to their legal protection under the Rights of Way Act, which came into force on 1 January 1934 – just as traditional rural life, when most people still walked or rode horses for transport, was beginning to decline. The number of private cars on Britain's roads doubled during the five years before and after this date, reaching two million by the outbreak of the Second World War, and their use spread exponentially from the mid-twentieth century onwards.

Before this time most people walked because they had to, or if they were on pilgrimage. With the rise of

Romanticism came the idea of walking for pleasure, prompting such poets as William Wordsworth in the Lake District and John Clare in the East Midlands to pen some of their finest words after traversing the landscape on foot. Two hundred years later, walking for the enjoyment of it remains deeply rooted in our culture, with 'a good walk' a time-honoured cure for many ills and the humble Sunday stroll an occasion not only to enjoy the countryside but to connect with our friends, family and community.

Following this bridleway, eroded to below ground level by centuries of footfall, brings a powerful sense of connection to the past – not only to my own past, but to the lives of those who have walked here since the time of the Anglo-Saxons. Their name for the assart in the forest that once covered these hills still survives: Esseleie, the 'clearing in the ashes', which mutated over the centuries into its present-day spelling, Ashley. 'Green' was a fifteenth-century appendage, marking the adoption of the common land used by villagers for grazing their animals.

Walking these paths, familiar to me from childhood – and likely still looking much as they would have done for generations before that – is for me a profoundly resonant experience. Far from breeding contempt, familiarity deepens my appreciation of the landscape; I notice each small change as the seasons unfold. It's late summer now, but only a few weeks ago the canopy above was tinged with the febrile new green of spring, the hawthorn hedgerows all creamy blossom. The scattered copses and woods, tender green and opaque with birdsong on my previous visit, have since darkened into the full maturity of summer. Blackberries are ripening on the bramble, and autumn is around the corner. The Chiltern beech woods will soon singe russet and gold, pink autumn cyclamen will cluster on the banks, and in the air will linger a portent that not only the day, but the year too is drawing to a close. Winter will come, and the chalklands will be at their most elemental. The ploughed fields then muddy to a palette of tawny browns, gleaming white with the flints from which, some 400,000 years ago, our forebears shaped the axes with which they hunted the game that once roamed these wooded hills. As I walk I feel part of a great unending cycle not only of the seasons, but of human connection with this place.

This state of close observation and connection – of meditation, even – is one I feel less keenly on unfamiliar paths. I'll notice what's around me, but not with the same granular attention to detail as when walking routes I've known all my life. This is especially true of my long-distance treks, when my attention can be distracted by the need to navigate, or I may be weighed down by the pressure to cover a set number of miles each day to reach my destination. On local walks, rather than passing fleetingly over the landscape, I form a relationship with it – one that is grounding, meaningful, and deeply restorative.

Many of our long-distance trails, such as the Cotswold Way or the Old Way, are essentially a patchwork of local paths, byways and bridleways stitched together, and so retain that texture of authenticity. You can follow them from village to village as people have always done, and still feel you're on a local walk. Other long-distance routes – the celebrated National Trails such as the Pennine Way across northern England, the Cambrian Way through Wales, or the Cape Wrath Trail in Scotland – are of a different character. They're modern inventions and not shaped by the patterns of everyday rural life. They don't exist to connect communities, as the old paths once did; instead, our National Trails are often treated as tests of stamina over difficult terrain, the miles covered each day clocked up on a fitness tracker. These are routes no right-minded villager of centuries past would have chosen, preferring instead the well-worn tracks that bound them to their fields, their animals, and to one another.

Unlike local walks, long-distance trails are often more about reaching a goal. And without straying too far onto the rocky terrain of gender politics, it's perhaps no coincidence that the majority of walkers on these trails, particularly the more arduous ones, are men. Often solitary figures, heads down, those that walk these routes can be seen striding across moors or mountains in silent competition with themselves. Few see anything heroic about walking domestic paths – those that radiate from your domus, your home. As the home, traditionally, was seen as the preserve of women – a feminine space and not one imbued with notions of adventure – domestic walks have typically been underrated. But walks from, and around, the home are of huge significance to many people; it is, after all, how many folk still choose to walk. And such walks enjoy undoubted advantages: there's no competition, no distance to complete, no new destination to reach. With just home to return to there's no pressure, no obligation. You are freer to linger, to observe, to reflect, or even to turn back without guilt. This freedom is especially welcome with Britain's famously unpredictable weather: you can seize a break in the rain without much planning, and beat a hasty retreat if the heavens open. They're walks of convenience and opportunity, and all the more precious for it, even if there's no renown accorded to those who walk in this way.

The tree tunnel opens out and the sky widens above me, a red kite's shriek evaporating on the wind. I come to an old farmstead, its steep tiled roofs lending it an almost East Anglian air. Once, this was a working farm. Built in the eighteenth century, it was alive with the clamour of labourers, the clatter of carthorse hooves, the squeal of cartwheels, the grunt of pigs. Now long-legged horses graze silently in its paddocks, and the timber-framed barn has been converted into a stylish home. Where the path once ran straight through the farmyard, a high fence now diverts it around the house and gravel drive, discreetly. Whether the occupiers prefer not to see muddy walkers traipsing past, or don't want the muddy walkers peering in at them, is not clear.

After the brief diversion, the path, bristling with nettles, slips back into the tunnel, the trees closing overhead once more. From the garden to my left a cockerel screeches – a timeslip to the village's rural past. Above, the faint scream of a jet engine on its descent into Luton Airport, sixteen miles away. The sound of England past overlaid with the noise of England present.

The path forks. Right, it leads back towards the lane and home. Left, it carries me deeper into the landscape, as the track becomes a holloway. This is a veteran path, eroded by centuries of water and feet, bounded by ancient hedgerows of native species: oak, holly and beech. From the Old English holh (hollow) + weġ (way), holloways have existed since the Anglo-Saxons first trod them, forging new paths to and from their settlements. History, especially medieval history, has been my passion as long as I can remember, and the knowledge that I'm literally walking in the footsteps of my forebears never fails to send a shiver down my spine.

The path descends, hollowing further until the banks on either side rise above my height, the air now cool, damp and musky. I come to a scrap of woodland, where a woman with a Labrador passes in the opposite direction. A beautiful morning for a walk, we both agree.

And here's another round of applause for the local walk. On long trails, where the destination is the goal, there's not often time to stop and chat, beyond a brief nod exchanged with someone coming the other way. Local walks, though, are a conduit for social interaction that not only supports your mental wellbeing but also fosters a sense of community. Even if an encountered walker is not a close neighbour, or is someone you've not met before, there's still an awareness of shared experience, of belonging. Importantly, local walks don't have to be rural. Most towns and cities contain green spaces

– parks, canals, nature reserves, even cemeteries – where people can walk and immerse themselves in nature and encounter others doing the same.

Local walks can also bring salvation. During the Covid lockdowns, when walks of up to an hour were permitted close to home, they became a lifeline for many of us. For people shut indoors for long stretches – and for those in flats, with no outdoor space – local walks offered both social connection and physical release. My husband and I would spend our daily hour of freedom exploring the paths round our house, rather than the more spectacular routes over the Yorkshire Dales we usually opted for, and found paths we never knew existed. We grew to love these modest yet companionable paths, and were almost sorry when lockdown lifted. With freedom comes choice, and too much choice can be overwhelming and sometimes disappointing. Bound by the limitations imposed during the worst of the pandemic, the domestic walks we were compelled to choose made us feel safe, and bonded to our home landscape.

Tramping these familiar local paths is like re-reading a favourite book. You know how the story unfolds, yet each time you walk them, you notice something new – a hidden rabbit burrow, or a rusting chain-pulled harrow half-buried in a field. Or a sign like the one before me now, which I'm sure wasn't here when I was growing up. 'Horse thieves beware', it warns. 'Our horses are protected with a Farmkey freezemark and can be identified by police'. A whiff of manure carries me back to pre-adolescence and a short-lived passion for horses, before those teenage years of school discos and pop-star crushes. The intervening decades collapse, and my nostrils fill with the aroma of saddle soap and the warm scent of the bran mash I fed my pony on frosty winter mornings. They say smell is the sense most powerfully linked to memory and emotion. For me, walking has the same effect. Each step I take along these familiar tracks imprints itself into my memory, lodged in my psyche as indelibly as the paths marked on the OS map.

For my villager forebears, who had neither Ordnance Survey maps nor modern hiking apps, memory was paramount. People knew every path of their parish, navigating by local landmarks. Church towers and spires, often the tallest buildings for miles around, served as obvious waymarks, as did natural features such as ancient trees – named as if they were people – along with hedgerows, streams and fords, hills and valleys. They used wayside crosses and shrines, most of these lost during the Reformation, and each parish would have had its boundary stones. On Rogation Sunday – the fifth Sunday after Easter, once the sowing of crops was complete – parishioners would walk the perimeter of their parish in a ritual known as 'beating the bounds' to ensure the boundaries were intact and fixed in memory. It's a tradition that continues in some parishes to this day though not, sadly, in Ashley Green, where the last Rogation walk took place in 2019 – curtailed forever by Covid.

Now, in walking this familiar circular route around my parish, I am committing these paths to memory. I am beating the bounds of my past life in this village. Like my predecessors, I'm impelled to check, each time I return to these paths, not only their continued existence but that my emotional bounds are also still intact. I'm connecting my past with my present, and in the knowledge that one day, when my widowed mother is gone, this long, uninterrupted thread will surely unravel.

At the confluence of paths, half-hidden by vegetation, a cluster of arrows points in sundry directions. I take the one leading into Butcher's Grove, an arm-shaped stretch of ancient woodland, of spindly beeches and sturdier oaks, the ground beneath stippled with star-of-Bethlehem. The bluebells of May have withered. These are not the delicately drooping, deep-purple native kind, but the taller, paler Spanish invaders. You rarely see Spanish bluebells in the woods near my North Yorkshire home, where our native flora is clinging on a little longer.

Out of Butcher's Grove now, onto a path skirting an immense field of wheat, perhaps half a mile square. Not a weed disturbs the rippling, pristine ears. Not a poppy. Not a cornflower – those lilac-blue blooms of the old agrarian landscape, named for the cornfields in which they once grew. The glyphosate-sprayed grain crackles in the hot wind like paper, and the grass at the field margins shrinks back, parched and brown. A butterfly lifts from the verge, flutters towards the wheat, then turns back. It's not in the modern fields that you find traces of the old Chilterns now, but in the edges, the verges, the borders.

Beneath my feet crunch flints churned up by the plough, and shards of blue-patterned pottery jut from the earth. In the centre of the field stands a lone oak, ancient and obstinate. Perhaps a dozen hedgerows were razed to create this vast sweep of monoculture, and so vanished the birds and insects that once lived in them. This tree alone was spared the bulldozer, perhaps to mark the old path across the field, which I now follow. And then, bending in the breeze, a single poppy, fragile, scarlet, defiant.

I follow the path across the wheatfield towards the woodland ahead, the lone oak my only waymark. Exposed to the full glare of the sun, I press on to its shade like a desert traveller towards an oasis. A pause beneath its branches to recover, before striking out again across the wheat steppe. The wood seems to recede like a mirage as I walk until, at last, I step into the dank, cool refuge of Crowfoot's Wood, named after the Middle English croufot, meaning buttercup. The path leads out of the beech wood towards a daub of green light beyond, opening into a meadow that in spring gleams with buttercups.

Even on a local walk, Chiltern country shifts constantly. It's country best seen, heard and felt at walking pace, as we trace the lives of our ancestors in the fabric of the landscape. You see it in the grown-out coppicing, and in the hedgerows with trunks bent and braided by hand in the old manner. These hills and valleys are a tapestry – elaborate, and in places threadbare – woven over centuries. Walking these paths for so many decades, I too have become a strand in that tapestry, a fragment of this village's history. It's just taken me a lifetime to know it.

*

There's another favourite walk that awaits me whenever I return to my home village. After turning right out of the driveway as before, and following the lane for a few moments, I turn right again, taking the path that runs opposite the old coffin route. It is, in truth, a continuation of the same approximate north-south line, crossing the lane at right angles – a typical four-way crossroads of the kind found anywhere along England's country roads. The lane where my parents' house stands was once a rutted track and is still called by its old rural name, Hog Lane (though there are no hogs living among the detached houses now). Today, the asphalted lane serves as a rat run for commuters – most of them paying little heed to the 30-mph limit – while the bridleway and path that crosses it has faded into gentler use, given over to leisure pursuits: walking, riding, cycling.

The footpath runs beside a high panelled fence, screening from view the large house behind. At its end is a metal gate – in my childhood a rickety wooden stile – which leads into the field beyond and feels, so many decades on, like a portal into my past. The next field, sloping down towards Hockeridge Woods, was where my younger brother and I tobogganed in winters when snow was still common, our father pulling the wooden sledge back up the hill until we grew too tired, cold or bruised to continue. The field is fringed with dense hedgerows where we'd breathe in the blossom of spring, build secret dens in summer and pick blackberries in early autumn. It was also the starting point of our Sunday family walks. Long after my brother and I had left home, our parents continued to walk here with our dog Holly and, after she was gone, on their own. Now, my father is dead, and my brother lives abroad. And unless my eighty-eight-year-old mother feels able to accompany me on the steep walk down to the woods, it's only me re-treading this childhood path, alone.

The Hockeridge Woods, riotous with birdsong in spring, are now summer-silent. To enter, you cross the bank and ditch surrounding the woods, dug centuries ago to keep out livestock. I head straight on, towards a medieval double bank and ditch crested with ancient hedgerows. This earthwork now marks both the northern parish boundary and the county line between Buckinghamshire and Hertfordshire, and, when we were still members of the EU, the Euro-constituency boundary between South East and Eastern England: a faint contour on the landscape revealing centuries of shifting jurisdictions, from parish to county to continent.

Unlike Butcher's Grove and Crowfoot's Wood, where native species still flourish, these are managed woodlands, with timber cultivated on a commercial basis. Once a tangle of oak and ash, holly and beech, the Hockeridges were gifted to the Royal Forestry Society in 1986 by Mary Wellesley, great-great-granddaughter of the Duke of Wellington. The woods had already been diminished and despoiled by mid-twentieth-century activity. Hundreds of trees were felled in the 1940s to help the war effort, and much of the mature beech forest was cleared by developers eager to expand the nearby commuter town of Berkhamsted. Rescued in 1952 by Miss Wellesley, the woods have been replanted with a wide variety of ornamental forest trees alongside the traditional species. Pride of place is given to a wide avenue of Wellingtonia – the English name for the giant redwood – planted in the 1950s by Miss Wellesley in memory of the Iron Duke.

As I approach the north-eastern edge of the woods, the growl of the new Berkhamsted bypass encroaches. I say new, although the bypass was opened in 1993, after I'd left home. But I still remember the silence of my childhood walks, when the only sound was the hush of the wind in the trees and the birdsong. I leave the woods at John's Lane, once a peaceful back road linking Berkhamsted and Ashley Green. It's peaceful no longer. Berkhamsted may have gained from its bypass, but it has come at Ashley Green's expense, with heavier traffic now spilling onto the main road through the village, and into its narrow, potholed lanes.

I turn right into John's Lane, the road dipping towards the parish boundary. Another sharp right brings me back into the woods, along Hockeridge Bottom. Otherwise known as Soldier's Bottom, this is the spot, according to local legend, where a battalion of soldiers once camped during the English Civil War, and where, it's said, their ghosts still march at dusk.

A little further along Hockeridge Bottom, an old agricultural roller sits rusting in a corner of the nearby field, long forgotten. Did its owner leave it there one day, intending to return for it? Or perhaps, seeing that the old rural life was slipping away, he knew he would have no further use for it. The path re-enters the woodland, where clusters of catkins dangle from the hazel hedgerow in spring. Revered in Celtic times as the tree of knowledge, hazel was believed to hold magical powers, and felling one was punishable by death. Once valued for making fences and hurdles, it's still used today in water divining. Perhaps its old magic will keep me safe from the ghostly soldiers, and from whatever else lingers in this uneasy stretch of woodland.

I'm still in Buckinghamshire – just, as the tract of woodland to my left lies across the border in Hertfordshire. My childhood in the village was lived mostly on the western side of this boundary, though I would cross the main road to my Church of England primary school, and later for awkward teenage discos in the village hall. The school building still stands, though the school itself closed in 1983 to become the village community centre, now home to Pilates, yoga and bridge classes. Yet all these years later I still remember morning playtime: cold knees, the third-of-a-pint bottles of faintly sour school milk and the comforting smell of polished wooden floors.

At the woodmen's cottages on the main road I turn right once more, back into the Hockeridges, along the old paths and the newer tracks churned up by logging vehicles. The path emerges again onto John's Lane at the lay-by where, during my childhood, every fine day an elderly couple would park a pale blue Morris Minor beneath a dome of beech, sitting inside their car with a flask of tea and a picnic lunch. Then it seemed a curious way to pass the time, but now I understand the attraction of silence, of stillness, of slowing the clock. And then, one day, they did not return. Like the curlews near my home in the Yorkshire Dales – whose arrival in late February I still mark as the herald of spring – their leaving went unnoticed. Spring merges into summer, and suddenly you realise you've not heard a curlew call for some time. They're long gone, away to winter on the coastal estuaries. Gone without fanfare, like the couple in the Morris Minor, whose existence on this Earth was almost as fleeting.

I turn left along the lane, then right, into a meadow. Unlike in the Hockeridge Woods, busy with dog walkers, I usually meet nobody here. I may be alone, but I'm not lonely. Chaffinches, rooks and pigeons call from Willow Wood. This remnant of old woodland sheathes the path for a short stretch, and though I search for willows, I see only beech, oak and holly – the bush considered protective to the Druids and later, for Christians, a sign of Christ's crown of thorns. Here, along a simple parish path, I'm reminded that even the most unremarkable of landscapes is layered with meaning, belief and symbolism.

Swinging right along the single-track boundary road, I pass Firs Wood – probably a corruption of furze, from the Old English word for gorse – its name echoed by Furzefield Wood on the opposite side of the lane. There's a sense of the day drawing in, and with it the instinct to turn back towards home. The path skirts Pancake Wood, where as a child I would fantasise about running away to live wild – if living wild were possible in the English Home Counties.

I cross the lane and take a shortcut along the southern embankment of the Hockeridges, radiant with forget-me-nots in spring. This embankment has always been my favourite woodland path, perhaps because it marks a small but decisive border between the seclusion of the trees and the sunlit fields beyond. It carries a deeper significance for me now, for not far off this path, around the roots of a lone pine tree, my mother, brother and I scattered the ashes of my dear father, who died four years ago. He had so loved these woods, where he walked for more than half a century, until extreme old age and emphysema made the climb back up the hill impossible. There's solace as well as sadness as I walk this familiar path, for I feel him here still, an eternal part of the place he never really left.

When I follow these old pathways around my village, I'm most certainly walking rather than hiking. In Britain, 'hiking' implies something more strenuous, through rougher terrain or over longer distances, much as in American usage. When I tell my mum, as I do each day of my stay, that I'm 'going for a walk', my meaning is clear: I'll be keeping it local, and I won't be long. I may pull on the worn pair of hiking boots I keep at her house, but I won't take a backpack, trekking poles or a map. She knows I'll be back in time for tea. But when does a walk become a hike? And when does a stroll along local paths evolve into a greater and more momentous journey?

On the third day after my father's death, I set out as usual from the house he had shared with my mother for more than half a century. This time I not only wore my old boots but also slung a backpack over my shoulders and packed an OS map. His death, at the age of ninety-one, had been expected, yet I was grief-stricken. And the only way I knew how to work through that grief was to walk.

On my wrist was the watch he'd worn every day, and which the nurses had removed so tenderly a few hours before he died.

Turning right out of the driveway, I walked along the lane that he'd strolled for fifty-three years, and down which the ambulance had driven him to the hospice where he spent the final thirty hours of his life. On that day I held his frail hand in the ambulance as it made its way along the lane and out of our village, watching the autumn foliage slide by. I knew my father would never see his home again, and I felt my childhood slip away.

Now, three days on, I continued down lanes flecked with yellow and gold, past bronzed bracken and hedgerows alive with sparrow song. Ash trees dripped their leaves, and skeins of pink and lilac braided the sky. I walked through the familiar beech woods – backdrop to my father's life – and across meadows jewelled with rain. Branches creaked in the warm wind, an autumn day that felt like summer. A crisp packet glinted in the earth, and squirrels darted across my path.

Crossing the parish boundary, I passed a ruined medieval chapel, overgrown and crumbling back into the earth, then on through stubbled fields where flints shone from the brown soil. From far off came the faint pop of shotguns – as if there were not already enough death in the world.

On through ancient woodland and along a leaf-strewn path where an elderly couple were gathering sloes, past the 'good mornings, lovely days' of dog walkers, and out across fields of winter wheat, boots squelching.

It had rained for two days following my father's death.

I strode past discarded corn husks, fallen like birds. On through woodland where my parents had walked for five decades, towards the roaring bypass that sliced through the trees, robbing the woods forever of their silence. The sky was raked with cirrus. I crossed the bypass and left behind the entrance to the hospice where my father had spent his last two days.

I paused to lift a frog lying motionless on the road, its small body still warm, and set it down on the verge. Then on to an ancient holloway, once trodden by farmers and drovers, travellers and traders, and the roar of the bypass faded to a whisper. Old hedgerows grown into trees knitted above my head, and a red kite mewed like a lost kitten. I walked on, down into a valley of mist, grazing horses, furrowed fields and burnished woods – the path becoming track, the track becoming road.

Over the brick bridge spanning the canal where we once took a family holiday. A decaying narrowboat, much like the one we had hired, lurched against the bank; the wind hissed in the reeds, and the intervening decades ebbed away.

Across the railway along which my father travelled for twenty-one years on his daily commute to London. The modern routes weave through the valleys; the ancient ways cross them. I climbed steeply up and out of the valley, along quiet lanes and leaf-littered tracks, then down again through beech hangars and ripened orchards to Aldbury. The Chiltern escarpment stretched ahead in a mosaic of gold and bronze.

I walked north along a narrow lane that hugged the escarpment, the trees weeping their autumn leaves. A fox flashed red across a field and the landscape opened as I climbed out of the valley. The arable gave way to the pastoral; sheep-grazed downland, not ploughed fields, now encircled the horizon. A red kite swooped low, twisting its tail like a rudder, while pied wagtails bathed in last night's rain.

A lone skylark sang the song of my childhood summers in the meadow behind our home.

I left the lane and followed paths across sheep-cropped down beneath pale blue skies. A young man with flowing dark hair and no shoes crossed my way, and told me he had been walking barefoot for weeks. I continued along chalk-white tracks and through woodlands of ancient oak towards Ivinghoe Beacon, the Iron Age hillfort where three counties meet. It was here that my father would bring us as children, to watch our paper kites lift into the wind.

The red kite swooped beneath me now.

The skies were darkening as I reached the beacon. From its summit I looked north to the flatlands of Bedfordshire, east to the Dunstable Downs, and south to the Chilterns of my childhood. Then I turned west, towards the setting sun, where the Ridgeway, Britain's oldest road, threads its way over the horizon. West, towards the place my father had been born almost a century ago, his long life just a short chapter in this land's history.

Somewhere, at an indefinable point along the way from our village to Ivinghoe Beacon, my walk had shifted from the local to something more. No longer a circular ramble but a linear route, it had become a journey. Each step of the way, as I placed one old, worn hiking boot in front of the other, carried with it memories of family, of childhood, of my father. And alongside these cherished people, I like to think that I was also walking with those who have passed here before me; perhaps, even, those who will come after.

Walking through Time

Anita Sethi

It's past midnight in Manchester and I'm about to set off on my daily mandated walk during the third national lockdown in England. It has been the longest, darkest winter. Unlike some countries where there are night curfews in place, we are allowed out past midnight for exercise – one of the 'reasonable excuses' for being outside, though the government guidance stipulates that this should be limited to once per day and that we should not travel outside our local area. Walking at such an hour can be both terrifying and terrific, with the streets eerily empty and only my own shadow for company. My hometown has become a ghost town. This is a time in which I have truly discovered the value and power of walking and, with no constraint on when I can take my one walk per twenty-four hours, I've been getting to know the night.

I am living in a hotel again, currently between places. From the landing near the lift I am looking out from a floor so high up that I can see, glowing over the city centre, the clock on the Kimpton Clocktower Hotel opposite. It is topped by a copper dome which has weathered to a delicate turquoise. The baroque clocktower is one of the most striking landmarks of the city, a tall eminence rising from a Grade II-listed building made of red brick and terracotta tiles. It was once the Palace Hotel, and before that a life insurance and pensions company. As the horrific daily death tolls from the virus continue to accumulate, I often watch the clock, my heart racing, wondering how long each of us have left. Tonight I look a while longer and watch snow begin to fall, white flakes tumbling past the terracotta, drifting through the darkness.

From this heightened view I can also see the train tracks, for the hotel I'm living in for now is right by the Oxford Road train station where TransPennine Express and Northern lines run frequently. I hear them at night, squealing through the city. Almost no one is allowed to ride them, but still they run. The ghost trains track their way through my dreams. A memory surfaces of the year before when I was racially abused on one of those trains; I try and let the recollection fade into the night. There's enough to think about as it is. Below I see a slick of black water beneath the railway bridge, for running through the heart of the city is the River Medlock, which I'm looking upon now, along with the River Irwell, the Bridgewater Canal and the Rochdale Canal. I feel a surge of excitement to be stepping down into this view, to be walking through it, into it, entering the city, letting it become part of me, and feeling myself become a part of it.

I leave my bird's-eye view behind and descend to human level, stepping out onto a street usually streaming with traffic but now empty and silent. A blast of cold air hits my skin and takes tears from my eyes, but the shock of cold night air enlivens me too and I put one foot in front of the other and walk. The pavement and road are becoming covered in snow, which is sticking and staying with so much more ease without the relentless passage of dirty wheels or human feet.

I look up and dustings of snow fall onto my face; the cold on my skin feels delicious. I watch the clockface on the hotel glow in the dark, round and moonlike. From here, I'm now gazing up at time, no longer level with it. If you peer closely at the clock on that huge clocktower, you will see that the hours are marked in the shape of bees, the symbol of Manchester signifying its industrial history: a city of worker bees.

The clock has stood there measuring the time for many years, with construction for the building of which it is part occurring in segments between 1891 and 1932. It was originally built to be the Refuge Assurance Building, but after the company moved out in the 1980s, the building stood derelict for many years before being converted into a hotel. That hotel, today sitting beneath the clocktower, is rumoured to be haunted – one of the staircases is said to host a grieving war widow who threw herself off the top-floor landing and died on the marble floor at the base of the stairs.[1] A room is also reported to be spooked by the sound of children playing at night. From my hotel room over the road, I have been reading up about the history of the place, including the hotel reviews – one visitor staying there shared how they left their room and on their return found a closet door open and possessions moved around. They had no explanation.

I know that deep beneath the hotel were a number of huge vaults and safes protected by iron bars. Where a restaurant now stands, once upon a time there was the typing room where there would be hundreds of clerks working on documents, insuring people's lives, with vast quantities of valuable documentation then stored in the vaults. As I walk, I'm haunted by all that lurks not only above the street, but what lives on beneath ground level, deep within the city's subterranean spaces.

I move through the city and feel the pace of time slow as I put one foot after the other. I've been so terrified of the passage of time these last few months. I've been so out of sync with the turning of the world in this lockdown, which has ruptured my relationship with my internal clock. *Keep time, keep time* – I walk and each footstep I take is a kind of time-keeping.

I walk on and stop to watch the river, which gleams black, gloriously black, and disappears into a series of underground secret passageways and little-known tunnels. My thoughts follow the water as it flows beneath bridges and I wonder about all that has been carried upon it over the years.

As I walk, an image surfaces in my mind of a painting titled *India House*, which I've seen when I've visited the Manchester Art Gallery. The painting looks down the River Medlock, and a dark archway, belonging to the railway viaduct on Oxford Road, frames the scene. India House dominates the image, its bright lit-up windows reflected in the water. The painting is by the impressionist painter Pierre Adolphe Valette, who captured scenes of Manchester, including the Medlock and the Manchester Ship Canal. In several of Valette's paintings, day and night are indistinguishable due to the smog and pollution filling the sky. In the absence of sunlight, distinctions of time are obliterated.

The painting flickers and fades in my mind as I pass on through real-life, present-day Manchester.

I walk and walk and pause and drink in the landscape – which in this snow looks something like a Lowry painting. As I walk, I wonder how I can capture this city and my perambulations through it; how walking its ways and streets can help reveal submerged histories.

The lights of the Victorian-looking streetlamps spill into the streets that now glisten with snow so delicate it appears as a fine sugar. The lights are the main presence here in these empty streets, in this city which became the epicentre of the Industrial Revolution that transformed the country. My hometown is one of the birthplaces of industrialisation: the first street in the world to have gas lighting was in Salford, Lancashire (now part of Greater Manchester), back in 1806.

As I walk through pools of amber light spilt by the streetlamps, I wonder what it would have been like to have lived through that transformation of the night. I wonder, too, about the lives of the people whose work made such transformation possible.

I pass beneath the bridges near the GMEX and see vast warehouses that for many years lay derelict, and which are now being transformed into trendy apartment blocks. Before they were destined to house young professionals, these warehouses held vast quantities of cotton, among other products. The cotton made the city famous as 'Cottonopolis', a great trading city of global importance whose significance relied on this imported material. As I wander by the warehouses, I think about the lives of those whose labour enabled Manchester to become rich from cotton: enslaved people working the plantations of places including Dominica and Guyana, who never saw, or reaped the benefit of, what was built with their work after the cotton they grew arrived at the foot of Quay Street.[2]

British hunger for cotton grew in the 1600s from the importation of South Asian decorated textiles. With established textile manufacturing trade links, Manchester started to expand, building more and more factories, creating greater demand for slave labour. As the appetite for cotton fabric increased, mill owners sought slave-picked cotton from plantations in the southern United States: by 1860, plantations in the US supplied almost 90 per cent of the cotton used in Lancashire's mills. In Manchester and many surrounding Lancashire towns, cotton was spun into yarn and fabric in mills by factory workers: men, women, and children as young as five years old working long hours in often dangerous conditions.

I find myself walking by the waterways of Manchester that bore the goods of slavery to the city. In 1734, the

River Irwell Navigation enabled direct shipping to the leading slave-trading port of Liverpool, while the Bridgewater Canal carried bulk goods from Liverpool to Manchester's warehouses. The world's first intercity line, the Liverpool and Manchester Railway, opened in 1830, transporting slave-grown American cotton from Liverpool's docks to Manchester's textile mills.[3]

I move on, and I am startled to meet Abraham Lincoln standing tall, still and solemn in the cold Manchester night. One of his arms is folded over the other and he gazes steadfastly ahead. I look into his face. Dear Mr Lincoln, how did it feel, I ask, to help the tide of history turn in a better direction? In this pandemic-silenced city, streets emptied by crisis, the bronze statue of this famous historical figure seems to become an almost real-life companion. So I listen out for Lincoln's reply, communing across the centuries. *Be sure you put your feet in the right place, then stand firm*, I hear, as a bird flutters nearby.

The Lincoln statue commemorates the support of the working people of Manchester for the abolition of slavery – at a public meeting at the Free Trade Hall on 31 December 1862 they expressed 'profound sympathy with the efforts of President Lincoln'[4] and sent an address to the president. I hear their words reverberate across the years: 'the vast progress which you have made in the short space of twenty months fills us with hope that every stain on your freedom will shortly be removed', they wrote. Upon the statue is imprinted a letter Lincoln sent in return, thanking the workers of Manchester for supporting him during the American Civil War by boycotting slave-grown cotton. The statue marks these moments of interchange, of solidarity. I'm standing here in this moment due to the unique circumstances of this plague-time I'm living through – yet I also stand in solidarity with what the statue represents.

I realise that as I walk I am walking back through the city's history to a time in which human beings were treated as property, as objects.

I continue on, but I am disturbed to run into a ghost of my ancestral past – William Gladstone. He stands looking out over the city, but unlike Lincoln's statue – which made me feel like I had encountered a companion – William Gladstone's makes me feel like I have met an enemy. It was William's slave-owning father John Gladstone who initiated the large-scale brutal system of starvation-wage indentured servitude that was intended to plug the labour gap following the abolition of slavery in 1833. My maternal ancestors endured this servitude.

The first shipment in what came to be called 'the Gladstone Experiment' saw 419 people brought to British Guiana from India on the *Hesperus*. Thirty-nine of these died and seventy became ill. On the Gladstone estate there were reports of beatings and salt being rubbed in the resulting wounds of the indentured labourers: deliberate cruelty. An investigation by the British government discovered that workers who had signed up for the voyage from India were trapped in a 'wretched condition'.[5] I want to know, amid all the greed and hunger for power and wealth, if John Gladstone ever felt a sliver of shame. Did he feel no sympathy or empathy for the plight of the labourers? For the horrific, degrading conditions they endured? As I stand on the silent Manchester street, I want to know why Gladstone decided to continue exploiting humans for profit even after slavery itself was abolished. Did he feel nothing? Or was his heart as hard then as the cold statue of his son is now, on this bitter midwinter night?

I look up into the face of William Gladstone, who inherited much of his father's wealth from slavery and indentureship, and I shudder to think how he has been proudly immortalised here in a statue, while the story of my ancestors is all but absent from history and certainly from public commemoration in this place. William Gladstone, I'm here now looking at you. I am a direct descendant of this horrific system of exploitation; my own maternal ancestors were 'Gladstone Coolies', shipped to the Caribbean from British India to toil on sugarcane plantations in what was then British Guiana.

I realise then that, despite growing up in this city, I had never even been aware of the Gladstone statue; a night-time walk is bringing to the fore what can be hidden during the day by a hubbub of people. While I welcomed my midnight rendezvous with Abraham Lincoln, I am troubled by running into Gladstone – indeed, staring at his statue, I feel a hot swell of indignation, rising into rage.

I turn my back on Gladstone and, as I walk away, I think of my ancestors. Perhaps they were kidnapped, as many indentured labourers were before being stripped of their freedoms and taken into bondage, or maybe they voyaged willingly in hope of a better life, only to meet exploitation on arrival in the sugar colonies. I think of them at the port in perhaps Kolkata or Chennai, before making the harsh journey across the seas to the Caribbean. Many indentured women were brutally beaten and raped by their masters, while the suicide rate among both men and women was extremely high. They also soon realised that they had been sold false promises, signed false contracts or been given no contract at all. They often had identity documentation confiscated, trapping them in the plantations, where they were subjected to punishing conditions. As I walk, I imagine the despair my ancestors felt. I wonder if they ever felt hope for the future, or if they would feel pride at one of their descendants trying to give voice to their history.

I walk and stop to watch flakes of snow fall onto the canal. Some melt and vanish, but further on, part of the canal is frozen and the snow settles. I look out over the waterways and contemplate all the vast swathes of history that lie submerged. How far is there still to go before all are treated as more than object, as fully human? How far is there to go to eradicate systems of exploitation?

I walk on and I see Emmeline Pankhurst ahead, her arm outstretched into the cold winter air, palm skywards, snow falling onto what looks like stony, silvery skin. I stop to say hello. Dear Emmeline, I ask the statue, what was it like for you and your daughters, walking through such an unequal world? What kept you walking forwards, struggling against a misogynistic system despite significant opposition, enduring imprisonment and police beatings? A whole conversation unfolds in my head as I approach the statue. I tell her, I was taught from an early age to revere you, saintlike, but only later in life discovered that you became increasingly conservative and began to expound views supporting racial supremacy, giving eugenicist speeches about 'race betterment'. You supported an empire that held my ancestors in indentured servitude. If you lived now, would you disdain me for standing here looking at you? Would you regard me as being too inferior to have the same rights as white women? I want to ask her. Would you converse with me as an equal? The statue gives no answer.

I cross St Peter's Square and I watch the snow settling on the bare brown branches of the great trees here. Emmeline Pankhurst stands across the square from the great dome of Central Library where I spent hundreds of hours during adolescence escaping into books. I would devour books before beginning to write myself, and since those early days, walking has been central to my creative practice – between study sessions in the library, I would walk around the city, as I am tonight. I would write and walk and write and walk and write and walk, and walking helped me to process all that I was living through, as it is tonight.

I walk on by the waterways and contemplate the legacies of intergenerational trauma which have moved like waves through history and into my own life. The lashings my ancestors endured left not just physical scars but emotional wounds, and the violence that filled my own childhood appears differently to me now: the legacy of a long and brutal history.

As I move, contemplating the geography of this city and its connections to other places, I wonder about the cartography of feeling. What of the emotions that seep through time and place, passed from generation to generation to me right here, right now? A feeling of 'unrealness', of being a ghost in my own life, far pre-dates the pandemic, and pre-dates terms such as 'derealisation', 'depression', 'complex post-traumatic stress disorder' – it's there in my earliest childhood, and I see it now as an effect of the pain of brutalisation and objectification. Now I see how it is part of the emotional legacies of indenture, of being treated as less than human – haunting the generations. In diaries now locked away in a storage space in Deansgate, Manchester, my childhood self describes 'feeling like a ghost'. Now it's back, that feeling of being like a ghost in this world – and little wonder, for it has been so long since I have physically touched another human being in this lockdown that I have found company with statues, with the ghosts haunting the city. It's as if I've crossed over into some other realm and am looking back upon a world that once was.

As I walk, I am also filling with a sudden longing for life. I see the river again and gaze into its dark watery heart that soaks up my longing. I gaze into it and feel a greater sense of embodiment, of connection, of being part of this urban landscape – and the nature running through it, these inky black rivers.

As I walk, I feel myself moving from ghost to living being, crossing through the threshold.

As I walk, I feel my heart beating stronger, the muscles of my limbs, the cold whipping against my skin and a gathering wind whirling around my ears.

As I walk and turn my face to the sky, I feel the snow on my skin, the coldness enlivening.

I walk myself into a state of re-embodiment.

I walk myself back to life.

And as I walk, I vow to remember all those who are no longer part of life, of history. I walk in the footsteps of my ancestors who toiled on sugarcane plantations, enduring cruel conditions, suffering beatings and lashings and rape. I walk in the footsteps of my Mancunian ancestors, too, united not by blood but by place, those who stood up for abolition, for a better world. I walk forwards, too, not in anyone else's footsteps but my own, each footstep freeing me from cycles of intergenerational trauma, each footstep mapping out new cartographies of emotion.

I walk not really knowing where I am wandering. I look down and revel in seeing my fresh footprints in the snow in the deserted city. It gives me a delicious feeling of starting afresh, of forging a new path. 'I am a slow walker, but I never walk back,' said Abraham Lincoln. While I have been shaped by my history, I understand that I am not doomed by it: I am not destined to repeat cycles of trauma. With the knowledge I have gained by walking along Manchester's streets, I know I can break harmful cycles and begin again. I stop and pick up a pebble and hurl it into the canal and watch it splash, making new ripples, new patterns, and I walk on, growing to understand how walking can create new ways of being in this world. As I move, I determine to write this down, this ghostly night walk I've done through Manchester, and share the spirit of my ancestors. I want to share, too, my rendezvous with the historical figures I've encountered along the way, as well as this strange time I'm living through and what a lockdown night walk has taught me. For through writing, I can somehow immortalise that which is inherently transient. These fleeting footsteps can forever be captured.

Walking Work

Beatrice Searle

The Whin Sill may be northern England's best-known rock formation. Set into motion 300 million years ago by the parting of tectonic plates, it was formed from a vast, slow tide of magma, eighty metres high in places, which intruded into its surrounding rock and cooled to immortally tough quartz-dolerite. The rock that once overlaid and ran alongside it has long since been weathered away to nothing, while the sill remains: quietly assertive and slow to give way.

* * *

It might be said that averting the fall is the constant work of being human. We are two-legged creatures, after all, and it is difficult, perilous even, to proceed without collapse. One foot floats through the air, tipping the body towards the ground, and we must place the loose foot as quickly and surely as possible to bring ourselves upright before the second foot lifts off and we are in danger again.

The more we slow this movement, the greater our chance of falling. There is a certain safety in making this motion at speed. But look. See how a slower passing of the feet produces a gentle rocking of the body from side to side that wasn't there before. It seems to me to be a clue to comforting the self, a means of rocking ourselves, a way to take charge of our own soothing. Maybe that is the work of being human perfected. If we have the courage to risk slowness, to slow even to the edge of falling, might that be the speed where respite is?

* * *

A long, guano-variegated bluff curves away from us. The gorse is twice my height, yellow-lit, pouring sweetness into the air as it warms. The flowers of the blackthorn are open but it's too early yet for leaves. It has been fourteen years since I last moved along this table of quartz-dolerite.

When, at twenty-one, I first discovered this path between Alnmouth and Dunstanburgh Castle, I had never before been the instigator or navigator of my walks; had never sought a path myself or walked solo, as I did here then. This path was the making of my adult walking, but my experiences here were not glorious, inaugural ones. At that time, when I was feverishly repeating this walk, there was nothing more to it than the desperate, essential using-up of adrenaline. Day after day my pattern was to pitch off the earliest train and bolt along this path as fast as I could. The point was to run away, to stay ahead of panic and the desire to strike my head against the wall again. Flight had the upper hand over fight, so long as my rapid motion along this path was not impeded. Either I could outrun the grief and bewilderment that pursued me, or I would surely be overtaken, as I had been before. I was aware of little as I fled through the miles but the relief of a danger diminishing.

Today is different. Today, I have cared to notice the spring here for the first time. Today, for the first time ever, I am not alone here. 'Stonechat there,' she says, 'see? Very rufous.'

The gains of my high-speed movement, fourteen years ago, were short-lived. They brought only a brief respite that had to be reinforced day after day. I was still so very far away from the knowledge of how to slow at all without collapsing totally. So I surged, stricken, along this path for months before the Whin Sill, the slowest mover in the scene, was able to infiltrate my consciousness. That intrusive body entered little by little while gorse, blackthorn, bird remained extraneous and unseen. The Whin Sill alone insisted and provoked, answered my desperate cry by echoing it back to me with a stony spin on it, providing me with the first of many stony models that would come to guide my life. I welcomed the intrusion, grateful that there still remained a chink within my soul for it to move into.

After many months more of flying obsessively and frantically along the Northumberland coastline, smuggling its whinstone into my heart, I finally amassed enough to drop. From total velocity to total collapse, the path had filled me up: I'd found my way suddenly to ground. When my mother received the call, my girlfriend, at the other end of the line, was clearly frightened. She said, 'I think you need to come, she just keeps falling on the floor crying.' My mother came, to my university city three hundred miles north, the moment she heard those words. She came the moment she knew. And finally an end was in sight. I wouldn't have to walk that way again, in the grip of such terrible speed.

Today the tabular layer of the Whin Sill is laid the same, with its fishing villages and fortifications. But a sea change has occurred. Now, fourteen years later, I am guiding my mum unhurriedly along a path where always before I had been frenzied and alone. 'Gimme a profile,' she murmurs happily, pausing. 'Are you a skylark?'

For many years she and I have talked about our desire to walk together, in this landscape that kept 21-year-old me from very great harm, and which later played a major part in launching the walk of my life, my five hundred miles along an ancient Norwegian pilgrim path, pulling a forty-kilo Orcadian stone behind me. When I began to write my account of that land-and-sea adventure, and my rich, unconventional relationship with stone, resolving through the writing all the ways that stone had answered for me, this first, formative Northumberland coast path could not be ignored. The Whin Sill had provided me with a stony example of resilience. Its stone had reached me, enticed me to see the sense and survival in aligning with and absorbing it. As a trusted reader of my early drafts, my mum and I were in step with one another as, bit by difficult bit, my writing process revealed the truth of my experience to us both. By the time I had grasped that writing could be my way to comprehend what had happened on those Alnmouth to Dunstanburgh walks, they were over a decade in the past. By the time I could offer my mum, fully and honestly, the truth and the extent of the jeopardy I had faced, it was too late for us to change the fact that I had walked here alone and desperately afraid of myself.

It is no wonder, then, that she feels great compassion for her child when she thinks of this place. It is the walk of mine that means most to her. More so even than my fifty-day walk across Norway with the Orcadian stone that taught me how to yield, to stay afloat, to move and shape-shift and to wield weight, the story of which eventually became my book. That Norwegian walk, Mum says, was a singular pursuit, impossible for most people and, as she likes to emphasise, very definitely impossible for her. But these ten miles in Northumberland, this humble day walk, this walk within her physical ability, is different. This lonely walk of which she had been unaware, this path of unimpeded, overwrought (e)motion that I had taken secretly, time and again. Having moved so very far away to attend art school, it had been easy to conceal my desperate walking habit and precarious mental state. The powerful instinct I felt to protect my loved ones meant that I kept my secret best from those who would fear most for me. If she had known back then how I was using this path, nothing would have stopped her from getting to me, from walking beside me.

With those days now so far in the past, our premise for coming here together today is uncomplicated. She is simply grateful for the rocks, the castles and the whin escarpment that offered me metaphors for making some saving-sense of my life, and happy to be seeing and touching them as I did. We feel no need to remake this path, towards which we both feel such gratitude, in a positive light. This is not a dwelling place of darkness and we are not pursuing some unfinished business. If we were, we might have accelerated the arrival of this moment, but in fact we have been relaxed about rescheduling this trip a few times as life, inevitably, threw other things our way.

But one particular life event allows and motivates my mum to walk with me here today, an event that has the potential to change the meaning of this path for us both. Her decision to step back from a successful forty-two-year career in arts fundraising has taken her more than two years to conclude. There has been much to come to terms with after so many decades of dedication: handovers to complete, explanations to give, fears to appease (many of them hers) and celebrations to share. Her first resolve was not to let this walk slide any further into the future. Only yesterday she finally left behind the familiar and safe pattern that she has been reinforcing since she was twenty-four, of major leadership roles with huge responsibilities and high targets in music, art and education. And today she steps onto a path new and unknown to her, with me.

She might not realise it, thinking as she does of this walk as mine, but she is front and centre here for me, at the heart of today. The timing of our walk here has given it a fresh purpose, charged it with something relevant and current. She has already enlivened and remade this path in anticipation, arriving giddy with her successes and recent celebrations, still fiery with passion for the arts and firm in her exceptional commitment, but peaceful and ready to embrace whatever comes next. Nevertheless, it has taken great personal bravery from her to arrive at this moment of retirement. It might be her intention to walk my walk today, but it is my greatest wish to walk hers, whatever it is going to become. So, for the first time, I am adapting my walking in order to share it with another. Though I am no longer a frenzied walker, my natural inclination is still for a long distance and a serious pace. This time we will walk in the slower spirit of the bird-watcher, with many a tea-drinking stop. I'll do more than just keep the sea on my right; for her I will consult the map and explain the stages. She has expressed some worries: a hip, a knee, an ankle might all let her down. All her clothes, including her boots, are newly bought for this moment. She is proud of the ankle-supporting way she has learnt to tie her bootlaces.

Despite all my experience as a walker, I am the one that looks like a liability today. My walking gear couldn't be scruffier. 'People are going to think you've fallen,' she says to me. But I'm foolishly fond of these walking clothes of mine. They are so well-worn, so far gone, that I am completely liberated in them. I don't have to modify my behaviour in any way to keep them presentable. My t-shirt, though clean, is permanently stained with suncream and sweat. It cost me only two euros because it is printed upside down, purchased for the picking of pink peppercorns on a dusty escarpment during my first Christmas in Cyprus with my husband's family. The wool jumper that I wear generously sieves the wind and is slightly shrunken so the sleeves come halfway up my forearms. I suppose it could still turn cold in these first days of April in Northumberland, but the outlook is good. The smells of sweating silage and sweet-sunned scurvy grass compete with one another, and the dunes radiate a thick heat. In the distance some toppled, concrete pillboxes halt her in her tracks again and she raises her binoculars to her eyes and asks me, 'What are those beached ancients?'

I have long been familiar with the romance of her words and from a very young age I took them all deeply to heart. For some years before I was eight, the breakdown of my parents' marriage meant that my mum and I did not have the regular time together that we longed for, so what I did have of her made a strong and lasting impression on me. In my childhood I knew of two great walks, and the first wasn't one I ever walked myself. It came to me only through my mother's stories of her time in Nepal in 1997. I was seven then, and from the moment she came home, describing stepped hillsides, tea with condensed milk, rose-petal paper and the smell of Himalayan pines, the thrill of walking became vivid in my imagination. Because of the evocative narratives with which she returned, and because I didn't have a great deal else of her to go on, I based much of my sense of my mother on those stories of her walks in the jungles of

Chitwan and districts of Pokhara. From that moment she was, to me, a committed walker.

I knew that she had been part of a small group that included her best friend, a honeymooning couple and a man with angina who was avoiding taking his medication, all led by Udhav, their Nepali guide. My mum has always been vulnerable to a kind of clothing claustrophobia, so she paired her sturdy walking boots with a long, loose-flowing navy skirt and wore a scarf in her pre-Raphaelite hair for dipping in rivers and cooling her head. Her stride was unrestricted, her motion unimpeded and her radiance, I imagined, total. She was a vision to me in those stories. Other Western walkers thought she was strange to dress this way, but she felt herself validated by the Nepali women she met on the paths. In their beautiful saris, she felt they noted and approved her skirt-wear. She loved to see who was on the path, and wondered for what purpose they were using it and what they carried with them. 'We all need the path to achieve an important thing,' she told me. She kept from me, still a child, her need of the path, but I did comprehend that for the Nepali women and children she met as she walked, the paths through the forests were routes to water, to food, to social life and education.

Udhav noticed that my mum was as keen a bird-watcher as he was, and as she walked up front with him and his young son, he pointed out the birds of Nepal to her: giant kingfishers, crested kingfishers, flycatchers and vibrantly coloured Indian rollers. 'I expected something extraordinary,' she told me, 'when he stopped dead, gasped, "Quick quick, come quick," and crept swiftly off the path and into the undergrowth, dropping down behind a rock. I followed and ran behind the boulder too. "It's a very rare bird," he whispered. So I looked and looked for a flash of rainbow feathers, but all I could see was a blackbird. Well, that was it. It was our common blackbird that he was so excited about. For all the birds of paradise he had in his country, a blackbird was the most exciting!'

As a pair of English blackbirds bounce about in the field we are passing, I remind her of this story.

'I've got a blackbird that sings Udhav's tune you know,' I tell her. 'And it's not the only one that does, we had one in Glasgow too.'

'Udhav sang that song to us all through Pokhara. It's a Nepali folk song, for safe travel through the mountains.'

'I remember.'

'Been to Nepal, has it, your blackbird?'

'I don't think they're migratory like that. But I swear it. It knows "Resham Firiri".'

Resham Firiri
My heart is flying like silk in the wind.
I cannot decide whether to fly or sit on the hilltop
Udera jaunkee dandaa ma bhanjyang, I sing
Resham Firiri, she returns.

When I was older I learnt that the trip had not been planned as a walking holiday particularly. Primarily it was intended to cheer up her struggling best friend, but

Mum was glad to get away too. She was facing some life-changing decisions and hoped that their big Nepalese adventure would quieten her mind sufficiently to make them. She was nervous about the walking elements involved; she hadn't much experience but had said she would be willing to try this new thing. 'I was no kind of walker at that point,' she told me. 'Walking had never been a possibility before. When we were children, Dad took the boys hiking. We girls stayed home with Mum. I was an adult, with agency, before I decided that walking would be a lovely thing to do, with my keen-walking friend, who was experienced but in need of my company at that time. The walks in Nepal were optional, day walks. In the end I joined every one on offer, though they tested me.'

So today I ask her, as we dodge the ragwort so as not to brush off cinnabar caterpillars: does she think of herself as a walker now? She tells me she doesn't. Only at very specific moments in her life has she walked with such intention. Walking for her is still unfamiliar, an irregular activity mostly accompanied by wariness. She was nervous before those Nepali walks and, though she invited them all, rose to the challenge and found each of them intensely wonderful, I can tell that she still lacks confidence in walking here now. I expect that she will experience our walk today in Northumberland as both meaningful and beautiful, in the same way that she thinks of her Nepalese walks, but she still won't think of herself as a walker.

'You are to me, though,' I say. 'Those stories from Nepal went deep for me. My sense of you as a walker is unshakeable because it was forged in childhood wonder. For me, your walking in Nepal was something of a principle you were founded on.'

Five years after Nepal came the second great walk, in eastern Crete. This time my brother, my mum and I would walk together. Crete was my first opportunity to become the walker I wanted to be. To my joy, my mum was wearing the same long, flowing skirt she had walked in in Nepal. We had planned to explore the Samaria Gorge but the week before we arrived it had rained relentlessly and the gorge was dangerously full of water. Our guide, muscular in her crispy trousers and Lycra t-shirt, threw the skirt a doubtful look but offered to lead us on an alternative route. I minded very much about the loss of a gorge, but was satisfied that we would still walk the promised nine miles. It was a bogglingly long distance, and I looked forward to this Cretan epic becoming my greatest achievement yet.

And so the walk got underway. It was Easter Day, and in the village squares communities were roasting whole goats. Red-dyed eggs were stacked in dishes. The elaborate ornament of Greek music trickled over the hillside. My mother moved easily, the hem of her skirt brushing the banks, sending the scent of thyme, mint and wild garlic high into the air. As we strode for miles along stony mule paths, faintly trotted goat tracks and between low tumbled-down stone walls, it became clear that the skirt was far from a hindrance to her walk or to anyone else's. It billowed its way to acceptance and then billowed to something beyond; it became unequivocally a respectable and much-admired item of walking attire within our group. Practically speaking, we all clocked a further win for the skirt – unfailingly convenient for a hitch up and a crouch down, easily and airily bestowing dignity.

Crete, when I was twelve, made tangible to me the wonder of walking, and greatly reinforced the sense I had of my mother as a capable and charismatic walker. I was proud that in her skirt she had proved all the doubters wrong, impressed them, even. She had been beauty and practicality personified. On the basis of the nine extraordinary miles we had experienced together, I felt confident that we three were now, irrefutably, a walking family. The herby fragrance of the skirt, hanging up in our hotel room, was a powerful and provocative assertion of this for the remainder of our holiday.

I have carried this conviction into adulthood. Now, examining it alongside my mum as we walk together for the first time since Crete, as we walk together for the first time in twenty-three years, I have to admit that as walkers we do not know each other well. Here we are at thirty-four and sixty-three, learning about the impressions we've carried of each other as walkers throughout that long time.

'Not in your skirt this time, Mum?'

No. Her sense of me is as a serious walker now. That is the understanding on which she's begun this Northumberland path. She's aware that this walk might be ambitious for her and wants to be 'well equipped'.

She cares to be 'appropriate', to do well in my eyes and not to let me down. Therefore it didn't cross her mind to wear a skirt this time. It seems she's never known that, throughout all my walking, flying desperately along in Northumberland and plodding steadfastly in Norway, pulling my rock, I held fast to my romantic idealism, to my idea of my mother in her long skirt as my walking archetype.

We stop again to fathom a vague shape down on the whinstone flats. 'Could be a sandpiper.' Competent with binoculars, she walks and sees completely differently to me. I am new to binocular-led motion. My chunky, handed-down pair of binos usually stay on the windowsill at home, much too heavy and awkward to carry around my neck, but I have them with me now because watching birds is one of my mum's loves and my plan is to walk her way today. My own binoculars seem to be bogus, bird-vanishing. They can never find the thing we are supposed to be looking at.

'Well, you've got one eye-piece out and one in.'

Oh. Well, I've got a clearer picture of the shore now, but I still can't transfer what I see with my bare eyes – the pointed rock beside the green pool behind the bird shape that we want – into these lenses. 'Hang on, yeah, I've got something… oh, no, not the right thing.'

We move off again and through two high thickets of gorse before a sound makes her exclaim, 'Linnet!' and we stop to find the source of the call. A potential eider duck halts us again a short while later. I have it in my sights and am preoccupied trying to focus the knobs on my binoculars when a man on the shore pops up in my near view and scares the life out of me.

Homing in on the shore life gives a purpose to the stopping, which I think Mum is glad of. I know that she would be embarrassed to be heard breathing heavily. I tell her that heavy breathing is encouraged, and I make sure to speak to her while breathless. Sometimes she stops just to say again, 'Sorry, this is magic.'

It's slow progress with binoculars. There is no sense of the momentum that I love so much and associate with a 'successful' walk. While she is looking at the birds and I am failing to find them, I am thinking instead of the way my walking here has evolved, from hurtling, blind, solo walks into this – taking pleasure in her stop-start pace, guiding her in all the ways I am able. She, in turn, is guiding me on our search for shoreline beauty. When first I walked here, I could not even have imagined trying the slower speed needed to find birds. As a result, I have literally never seen birds here before. Birds didn't get a look-in because I could not see anything until I saw the sill. And now… This curlew is abnormally, awesomely close. It is a bit surprising to have this kind of access, an unnatural proximity to the goings-on of the shingle. I have brought what is quite reasonably going on 'out there' right in here, up to my face. Here are the birds of the foreground, the near distance and the far distance delivered to me, filling my heart. My mum has enabled that possibility, through her company here today and her own particular walking preferences.

When I first told my mother, after much wrangling and examination of what was possible, that I would not, after all, be alone on my walk through Norway with my stone, she was relieved. Walking alone has never appealed to her, for herself or for those she loves. Her mind goes to the 'middle of nowhere': an encounter with someone or something nasty; the need for a rescue. She fears not only for me and for herself but for every solo walker, coming to walking late as she did and not having started when she was 'young and daring'.

'I own that that's a sad thing, but it's not a major downer in real terms,' she says. 'I want all the benefits of a quiet, solitary walk, often just to creep along quietly to spot the birds, but I feel the security of a companion and the beautiful intimacy of a shared experience as well. So I'll choose my walking and who I walk with very carefully. You have to be close to someone to walk away from them.'

When we stop for lunch the tide is out and a lone rock in the wet, sandy flat tempts us to perch on it. There are a few little residual pools at our feet and she doesn't want to get her new boots salty, so she muddles her way onto the rock. She is unschooled in rucksack etiquette, forgets to zip up the top compartment so that all the contents flop out as she moves her bag around to find her sandwich. She has not assigned categories of belongings to compartments, so the sandwich is not easily found. It is windy. Crisps are blown out of their packets and half the time I am chewing my own hair. But we persist on the rock because the view out to sea is completely unobstructed and so beautiful.

When some dog walkers wander near, she remarks quietly, seriously, 'Don't come here, this is the front row,' and makes me laugh. Before we move off, I mention that she might want to untwist her chest strap.

There is a pattern to my walking that comes from having once been a stone mover. I spent fifty days walking in the space between two pulling handles and harnessed by a climbing rig to a rolling wagon on which I hauled a weighty rock across Norway. Now I cannot walk anywhere without remembering my vital negotiations with the path. No matter how easily I am covering ground, I still quickly assess surface terrain and camber and judge how I will tackle the path as though I still have a huge stone in tow. I'm doing it right now; I've just geared my body suitably for a bit of a rush down onto slippy, shorn grass as though bracing for a huge, stony inertia. I feel a delicious satisfaction in 'still having it', the stone-moving sense. I let Mum in on this game, and as our walk goes on, she sometimes asks, 'How would this bit have been with your stone?' I tell her how the brief climb we did on a wide, well-trodden grass track to get above Alnmouth was gloriously suited to stone pulling. Twisting through the dunes, slipping down dry sand banks, finding a fair grip on the cracked bracken, that section would have taken more focus; many turns and switchbacks were not easy with a loaded trailer. The way we have freely deviated off the path to drop onto the beach and look for whinstone pebbles, then scampered along an anticline whaleback fold in the limestone – out of the question. I've been convinced, ever since Norway, that memories held by our physical bodies are uniquely safe. My body remembers, absolutely, when it hinges to go uphill or when I smell running freshwater, what it was to walk cross-country with a stone. My body's record stays true to the memory of stone moving, *truest* even, because, remarkably, it is the stronger habit of movement even here, where I used to move so differently. My old, urgent motion, all of it practised in this place, is overwritten, disregarded in favour of the productive motion that came afterwards. Panic couldn't keep a hold on my body like stone moving has. In fact, I am so changed on this return to Northumberland that the experience of following in the footprints of my younger self is eluding me somewhat. Mum is keener on it, closer to it. Sometimes she sends me ahead so that she can deliberately put her feet where mine have been. She is reassured by our companionship here, now, where previously I had none. I think she is proud, too, that her daughter wrote a book about walking and here we are together, doing just that and she is learning from me.

'There's a gannet,' I say. My eyes snap to it. A bird sighting of my own! What a pang a gannet's brightness produces. The sight of it makes me ache with longing for a way to describe it. For a few moments we both gaze skywards. When I eventually pull my eyes down, I notice, suddenly, how all that rescued me fourteen years ago is laid out in this scene. I must show her how perfectly framed this moment is. There, in the distance, is the whippy, red sandstone castle on its portion of obstinate whinstone;

immediately beside me is the great trapezoidal North Sea and in front of me is the next section of the coast path, and her standing on it. She has gone on a little way, but I've slowed again and stopped to take it in. And this time she is waiting for me.

I do not know when I will walk this path again, or if I will ever want to. It is ours now, and perhaps that is how I'd like to keep it. The air is tangy with the smell of kipper oil. I think the skylarks are throwing their voices.

As my mother and I part and return to our lives, I am about to embrace a new, very distinct type of walk. Back home in middle Scotland, a small working cocker spaniel waits for me to scoop her up. She is nine weeks old now, ready to come to her new home. Determined to do right by her, I have been in training. I have taken to heart the advice of our spaniel expert about this working breed – she wants to be at work while she walks.

I get it. As I imagine this little example of walking work rushing around my ankles, I realise that walking work has become non-negotiable for me too, though the puppy and I have different ideas about what this entails. I'll do her style of walking work with her; I won't ask her to do mine. I'll give her my full focus and together we'll hunt and we'll retrieve. Those are the jobs she wants to do. I'll try to align my thoughts to hers, to imagine only what it is to be a working spaniel. And as for my own walking work, I'll assign it its non-spaniel time.

Walking does its good work on me and, as a result, I have done good work while walking. My first and best work, the transformative work of pulling a stone, that allowed me to overcome real adversity, was kindled while racing along the Whin Sill. I have successfully built on that since; it has become natural to me to let my creative thoughts gambol along with my feet, further than they could in any other circumstance; to resolve thought, tender words and fragile ideas of writing, cutting letters, making sculpture, by putting one foot in front of the other, slow enough now to notice what surrounds me. Now I am convinced that part of the power of walking for me is that walking is an intuitive place to work. Though I walk less urgently, less dangerously now, still I know that my creative work is the way I can triumph over anything and that walking is the first step to finding out *how* or *what* to make. I can walk my way to discovering what I should do with my language and my hand skills; I can walk my way to finding the idea that is redeeming in every experience. Walking is, to me now, a considerable act of self-love.

Symperilambano

Katharine Norbury

'You have to move.'

'What?'

'You need to move. You must start walking!'

I was in The Bridge Theatre, by Potters Fields, on the bank of the River Thames. The show was an immersive production of Shakespeare's *A Midsummer Night's Dream*, directed by Nicholas Hytner. In a reversal of their traditional roles, Oberon, king of the fairies, had been tricked by his queen, Titania, into falling in love with a *rude mechanical*, Bottom the weaver. The hapless Bottom had entered the woods earlier that evening in the company of his friends. The group of young apprentices were hoping to perform a play the following night at the marriage of the Athenian king, Theseus, and the captured Amazon queen, Hippolyta. Oberon, having woken in his bower from an enchanted sleep, was just now pole dancing on a blossom-strewn four-poster bed to the delight of Bottom, whose human head had been replaced by that of an ass. Oberon's bed, and all who were in it, was making a circular lap around the auditorium and we, the people, were invited to follow it.

Movement stewards, one of whom was my daughter, were wearing boiler suits (in a gesture to the rude mechanicals) and purple flowers in their hair (in a gesture to the medicinal plant which had so affected Oberon's libido), and they encouraged – or, rather, instructed – the approximately three hundred audience members present on the stage to follow the four-poster bed. But it was no easy task.

'You *have* to walk!'

It was extraordinary how hard it was to get folk to move, even when they had bought a ticket for an immersive production, which meant that they, the audience, were immersed within that show. Most were delighted to be asked to perambulate behind the bed, and did so. Some started well, but then tried to slip into the centre where they could watch the action from a static position like wallflowers at a dance. The unexpected human island thus created caused a metaphorical logjam, around which two streams emerged: those who were happily walking behind the bed with a spring in their step – looking for all the world like figures on a Grecian vase – and those who had slowed their pace to a degree whereby the bed was rapidly catching up with them, and threatening to crash into them from behind.

'If you don't move you'll be hit by the bed!' an exasperated movement steward pointed out.

In the twenty-first century we have grown accustomed to a theatre's audience being static. Actors, for the most part, walk, dance, sing and fly before a stationary, seated crowd. The three visible sides of the performance space are protected from spectators by an invisible fourth wall. Us, and them. But it wasn't always like that. Contemporary theatre's forebears, the mystery plays – which date back to medieval times – were a way to share the stories of the Bible with a community who neither read nor wrote. These plays happened outside. Often they were situated next to churches and took the form of a tableau, and the actors might be clergy or guildsmen or other members of the community. As time went by and the plays evolved, and church politics with them, troupes of actors would travel with a wagon which served as a stage. There were no chairs. The landscape was the set. The audience used their ears and their eyes, their memories and their feet to follow the drama taking place before them. The people were, momentarily, fully present. When a scene required the presence of a multitude, the audience quite literally stepped up. Even when the first commercial theatres opened in London, there was plenty of room in the pit, the area in front of the stage, for 'groundlings'. The flow of energy between audience and players was fluid, more porous, more immediate, than we are largely accustomed to today.

This immediacy, this energetic exchange, was a day-to-day reality for Shakespeare and his contemporaries. Standing, wandering, shifting, and following the action on foot is still possible today as a groundling at Shakespeare's Globe Theatre on the South Bank of the River Thames.[1] In the immersive space of The Bridge

Theatre, just a mile downstream from the Globe, up to four hundred unseated members of the audience can be accommodated within the performance space. Those who stand – those who walk – are folded into the play in an organic, inclusive embrace. The fourth wall isn't such a solid thing for groundlings. They are watchers, distinct from players, yet are a dynamic part of the whole. The play's success is shaped by their presence, and by the level of their engagement. At the close of *A Midsummer Night's Dream* that night, Robin Goodfellow, known also as Puck, dropped backwards from a trapeze from where, suspended upside down, he reached out his hands:

So, good night unto you all.
Give me your hands, if we be friends;
And Robin shall restore amends.

With which words he reached for the outstretched hands of the two people nearest to him.

My interest in *A Midsummer Night's Dream* rests not simply in a love of theatre. It reflects also a fascination for magical spaces. Places where laughter and comedy, tragedy and farce, clowning and acrobatics, poetry and song, can remind us of another place. By which I mean a different space, a memory of which persists – although not necessarily as a recollection of something we have ever, in actuality, experienced. It is, instead, a notion – perhaps a dream – of something, or someone, or somewhere, that one has never consciously known. Despite our post-everything sensibilities (post-Reformation, post-Restoration, post-Enlightenment, post-Dualism, post-Rationalism, post-Industrialism, post-Modernism, post-Digitalism, post-Truth, you can add your own, the list is endless), we may, if we really look for it, still access this place. Its entrance lies within us. We each have our own ways of finding it.

A Midsummer Night's Dream begins with the announcement of the imminent marriage of King Theseus to Hippolyta. This would be the self-same Theseus who confronted and destroyed the Minotaur by walking into the heart of the Cretan Labyrinth in order to save the youth of Athens from slaughter. And who, aided by Ariadne's legendary ball of flax, was able to retrace his footsteps through dark and turning passages back into the upper world and daylight. In Shakespeare's play we inhabit a wood instead of a labyrinth and the head of an ass replaces that of the bull. But the means by which the young Athenians navigate the challenges of the night is, like Theseus before them, through the restless and constant use of their feet.

Never so weary, never so in woe,
Bedabbled with the dew, and torn with briers,
I can no further crawl, no further go;
My legs can keep no pace with my desires.
Here will I rest me till the break of day.

In the years since the Covid-19 pandemic, interest in the idea of pilgrimage, not necessarily for religious reasons, has flourished. The historian Tim Guile describes pilgrimage as a devotional practice involving an extended journey with a significant destination in mind.

The experience is short-lived, and while undertaking it the pilgrim is temporarily removed from their usual environment and identity. Both the physical and the spiritual, Guile notes, are blended into a single, unified experience. This might just as well be a description of the journeys of the characters displaced by their wandering in the woods outside Athens in *A Midsummer Night's Dream*. Hermia's words might easily be those of a contemporary British pilgrim.

A couple of years ago I attended a service at a church at the tip of the Llyn Peninsula in North Wales. The poet R. S. Thomas had been vicar of St Hywyn's during the middle years of the last century. It was the same spot where medieval pilgrims would have celebrated Mass before commencing the short but perilous, sometimes fatal, journey to the whale-backed hump of Ynys Enlli/ Bardsey Island, situated some two miles off the coast across the Swnt Enlli or Bardsey Sound. Its Welsh name means the island of the currents, or tides. The English name means island of the bards, or poets. A Christian community was established there around 516 by St Cadfan, although it may have provided refuge for persecuted Christians before then. In medieval times it was believed that three trips to the island granted the equivalent indulgences as one trip to Rome. It was said that if a person were to die there then Purgatory could be avoided altogether. This had the effect of encouraging thousands of pilgrims to make their way on foot to the tip of the peninsula, and from there attempt the journey to the island, some (though this may be a myth) carrying their coffins on their backs. It is still known as the island of 20,000 saints.

On this particular day the scattered nature of the congregation served as a reminder to visitors that the 'social distancing' rules, which had been imposed during the 2020 pandemic, were either still being observed or else had become a habit. White light illuminated the church – the reflected brightness of the sea beyond the cemetery wall. A wooden door banged shut. A faded reproduction of Rublev's icon representing the three angels at Abraham's table, sometimes taken to signify the Holy Trinity, hung from one wall. I looked about at the congregants, found my place. The vicar delivered a sermon focused on the meaning of a particular Greek word, which had apparently been inadequately translated. They explained how we should understand this passage of scripture in the light of this particular interpretation. My attention drifted to the icon. It spoke, and yet was silent. The artist was present, and yet long gone. The significance of the icon's colours, its geometric shapes, circles, squares, a triangle, the mystery of there being three angels, yet four places at the table. A place for Abraham? Or a place for you, the viewer, invited across the centuries to take part in the feast before you, represented by a tiny ox's head resting in a cup in the centre of the table. A building. A tree. The direction of the gazes of the angels, their gestures. Their silence. Their invitation to enter their reality. There were as many interpretations of the icon as there were observers able to see it.

The sermon was over. The congregation turned their attention to their service sheets. I had the sudden sense of being on an archaeological dig, brush in hand. I was acutely aware of being in an ancient and sacred space. But something was missing. It was as though we had lost or broken something of the most essential value. Either that or it was there, but we could no longer see it. Heads were bowed not in prayer but because people were following words on a page. It was as if what we held in our hands had been pieced together, perhaps over many decades, by an army of archaeologists, assembled from tiny fragments, using words so precious that no one dared lift their eyes away from them. The meaning of the words non-negotiable. It was as though we had discovered a miraculous, long-buried theatre, and were attempting to recreate what once had been. I imagined actors on a stage, a brilliant set, superb and skilful lighting. Yet the audience sat with their heads bent over their scripts, following the play with their fingers. How different it might have been if we had learnt our lines, knew them by heart, and were able to look up, and out, instead of down.

The sensation passed. The service ended. Some of those in the congregation were pilgrims on their way to the island. Over coffee and Welsh cakes they told how the path had led them from Basingwerk Abbey near Holywell to this church at Aberdaron. Tomorrow, weather permitting, they would travel to the island.

The total distance of the walk is 135 miles. It usually takes people about two weeks to complete it, if one averages ten miles a day, though others might attempt it in a week. The pilgrimage isn't as straightforward as it might have been because there aren't many places along the route in which to stay. The precise details of the path itself have been obfuscated as old buildings disappeared, their stones repurposed in field walls and houses. New roads cut through the place where the old path might once have been. The modern route is, in reality, a reconstruction. Our family had spent many holidays in this area and over the years I had watched the number of pilgrims to the island grow. I have not yet felt called to walk alongside them, though I have visited the island several times. Ironically, medieval pilgrims may well have received a more hospitable reception than their twenty-first century counterparts because what they were doing was considered normal then. Only the previous day I had met two sodden *pellegrini*, although there was no sign of them today. Perhaps they might arrive tomorrow. Those pilgrims had entered the post office in a village about a day's walk from Aberdaron. Staggering under enormous backpacks, they had enquired if there was anywhere they could get a cooked breakfast, or even an uncooked breakfast.

'No,' the postmistress replied.

After finishing my own business at the post office I had caught up with the pilgrims. I pointed out the places where they could find something to eat, and enjoy good coffee, and gave them my number in case the suggestions proved futile. The pilgrims' spiritual journey was routed through a largely secular community that had not yet fully awakened to the possibility of worldly rewards, by which I mean financial rewards, of providing affordable succour, B&B, a shower and a meal, to the wanderer. This was not yet the Camino Santiago, with its welcoming scallop-shell signs, indicating that pilgrims were welcome, and could find each night a cheap meal and a glass of wine and an affordable place to lay their heads. And yet, with each new set of footprints along the route, the way was becoming embedded, worn into the land. Like neural pathways reawakening ancient memories after a traumatic brain injury, or after a period of extended amnesia, the old and the forgotten ways were gradually re-emerging. But, as with immersive theatre audiences and studious church members, for it to work, those who are bystanders must also know their part and willingly embrace their role.

Give me your hands, if we be friends.

To return to the place where we began, and *A Midsummer Night's Dream*: the play is at one very superficial level about ordinary people who go walking in the woods and the transformations that occur as a result of that activity. None of them are walking without intention. The two sets of lovers are either seeking one another or fleeing from enforced marriage. Or both. There are the rude mechanicals, the Athenian apprentices who have left the city to rehearse their play in secret. And there are the fairies, inhabitants of a different realm that exists alongside our own. Their king and queen, Oberon and Titania, have come to bless the nuptials of King Theseus and Queen Hippolyta. Our guide in this forest is Robin

Goodfellow, or Puck, an amoral and whimsical sprite, who has created havoc through the hapless application of a love potion. We, the people, might be thought of as the trees. Puck, Oberon, Titania and the fairies are invisible to the mortals in the wood. That is, until Bottom finds himself with an ass's head in lieu of his own, during which time he is able to perceive the fairy kingdom and all those who live in it.

As the long summer night moves towards dawn, a fearful Robin Goodfellow observes the ghosts, including those of suicides, returning to their graves. There is little time in which to rectify the mischief of the night:

My fairy queen,[2] *this must be done with haste,*
For night's swift dragons cut the clouds full fast
And yonder shines Aurora's harbinger,
At whose approach ghosts, wandering here and there,
Troop home to churchyards. Damned spirits all,
That in cross-ways and floods have burial,
Already to their wormy beds are gone.

But Titania reassures him:

But we are spirits of another sort.
I with the morning's love have oft made sport,
And like a forester the groves may tread
Even till the eastern gate, all fiery red,
Opening on Neptune with fair blessed beams,
Turns into yellow gold his salt green streams.

Most weeks, when I can, I walk with my friend Trev in Banstead Woods in Surrey. We usually walk in a circle, as the woods are surrounded on all sides by fields. I suppose it is a pilgrimage of a sort. Trev is a priest, and our conversation often tends towards the spiritual, while the changing seasons and the miles passing below our feet ensure an unbroken connection with the physical. With the 'now'. The woods would already have been there at the time of Shakespeare.[3] They would already have been ancient. They are said to have been gifted by Henry VIII to Katharine of Aragon, and subsequently to Anne Boleyn. Sometimes, as we pass among the dog walkers and joggers, I imagine ladies in velvet, with dogs and falcons. Horses. Once, an antlered, black-eyed deer crashed past us, followed by a huge white lurcher; the dog was like something that had leapt out of a tapestry but for the muzzle and the radio tracker on its collar.

But we are spirits of another sort

The same oaks and yews that we walked beneath would have been there at the time of the queens. What now remains of Anne Boleyn is in an unmarked mass grave beneath the little church of St Peter in Chains in the grounds of the Tower of London. The church tower is clearly visible from The Bridge Theatre where this story began. But this isn't an essay about Shakespeare or church practice or the whims of tyrannical kings. It's a personal exploration of the relationship between movement and understanding, text and spirit, connection and embodiment, and about the idea, the inkling, that something has been lost.

In relation to both theatrical and religious practice something was, of course, lost. There was the most terrific hiatus in the years following Shakespeare's death. In September 1642 the theatres, all theatres, were closed as civil war swept the land, and they remained so for the next eighteen years. Actors were persecuted, fined and arrested until, at least externally, they stopped being actors. Within church practice the changes were already well under way when *A Midsummer Night's Dream* was first performed; the enforced marriage of Hippolyta to Theseus and the proposed forced marriage of Hermia to Demetrius (which caused the lovers' flight into the woods, with death as the penalty for disobedience) provided a way of exploring, without giving a name to it, the bleak and patriarchal landscape of the Puritans. Everyone knew somebody who was one. Shakespeare's eldest daughter Susanna was married to a Puritan doctor. Nicholas Hytner's new production at The Bridge acknowledged this uncompromising world by introducing the play with a grey-frocked, straight-faced, psalm-singing choir. (For some reason the Puritans didn't mind music, as long as it didn't happen in a church.) Pilgrimage, the very idea of it, was forbidden, and there was nowhere left to walk to in any case: the shrines and monasteries had already been dismantled. Statues and relics were burned or smuggled out of the country awaiting happier times. Indulgences, for the full or partial remission of the punishment for sins, and the nominal reason people set out on foot, were abolished. Mystery plays fell out of use, for the twin errors of involving both actors and forbidden doctrine. It wasn't until 1656, while the ban was still in force, that Shakespeare's godson, William Davenant, had the audacity to stage an all-sung play, *The Siege of Rhodes*, in his home.[4]

And as for the fairy realm? Those *spirits of another sort*? They were quite gone. The collective imagination had been purged with the same gusto as the theatres, the pilgrim routes and the churches. Although shoots were waiting in the dark earth, even if it was a while before they saw the light of day. In 1815 Walter Scott published a collection of papers that had first been assembled in 1691, thirty-one years after the theatres reopened. Scott called it *The Secret Commonwealth or an Essay on the Nature and Actions of the Subterranean (and for the most part) Invisible People heretofore going under the names of Fauns and Fairies, or the like, among the Low Country Scots as described by those who have second sight, 1691*. It was republished in 1893 by Andrew Lang and is a collection of folk tales collected by a Scottish church minister, Robert Kirk. Kirk had died, under somewhat mysterious circumstances, the year after he completed his manuscript, at the age of forty-seven. Curiously, at the time of his death, Kirk was out walking, late at night, dressed only in his nightgown, on what was regarded to be a fairy hill adjacent to his home. According to legend, Kirk's body was subsequently spirited away by the fairies either for giving away their secrets, or in order that he might become chaplain to the fairy queen, who I suppose must be Titania. Kirk's manuscript is full of first-hand accounts of what he called 'non-human spirits' and the phenomenon still known as 'the second sight'.

Which returns us again to *A Midsummer Night's Dream*, and to the secret commonwealth described there. To The Bridge Theatre, and the last moments of this lovely play.

Standing in the pit, I looked up as Puck swung gently from his trapeze. I was just behind him, his dirty feet catching in the fractured light from the spotlight overhead, the fur on his leather jerkin floating like feathers in the slight breeze of his movement and the thermals. I looked around the dark theatre. Perhaps a thousand pairs of eyes were focused on this charismatic sprite. I was in the presence of a mystery. Is mystery defined as that which cannot be expressed in words? Something impossible to articulate or understand? And he was speaking:

If we shadows have offended,
Think but this and all is mended:
That you have but slumbered here
While these visions did appear:
And this weak and idle theme,
No more yielding but a dream,

I wanted the moment to last forever. In a couple of days the show was coming down. This moment could not be repeated. Later, I would drive through the night for an appointment in the north of England. I was only here now because my car had had a puncture and I'd had to delay my departure. I knew that my daughter would be in the show that night, so I thought I'd go to the theatre to see her.

Gentles, do not reprehend:
If you pardon, we will mend.
And as I am an honest puck,
If we have unearned luck
Now to scape the serpent's tongue,
We will make amends ere long;
Else the puck a liar call.
So, goodnight unto you all.

And in that moment I realised what was about to happen. I caught my daughter's eye and she smiled. Puck dropped gracefully backwards, those strong ankles and dirty feet anchoring him to the trapeze. And I was looking straight into that impish face. An actor, yes, but a spirit, too. *A spirit of another sort.* I walked forward into the space and held out my hand. And he took it.

The Water of Leith and the Goddess Who Lives in the Mind

Anna Fleming

Out of the door, cross the courtyard, weave through the parked cars to pass through the old school gates and then over the cobbles to the riverside. It's hardly a grand beginning, but everything must start somewhere.

This is the daily walk. The easiest, most convenient way of rolling out of my flat and stretching my legs before starting work at the writing desk.

Passing the brambles, nettles and a girl on roller-skates, I look up and down the path, hesitating. Should I go left, downstream – past the spot where the man feeds the pigeons and the bench where the Polish sit with their cans – out to the shore and the harbour?

No. I need something longer today. A softer route – something greener – more meandering with more room for ease and flow.

Turning right, I walk upstream. The willows wave in the wind and underneath the road bridge, my feet slowly warm to the tarmac. But something feels off. I'm dragging my feet, struggling for rhythm. There's no spring in my step today, no sparkling thoughts, no vital energy.

What's wrong? I ask myself beneath the lime trees, by the dog walkers and Leithers idling on the benches. Nothing, really, the little voice answers, all perfectly normal. It's just morning, midweek, and a touch mundane, the voice grumbles. I've walked this way a thousand times before.

At the bend in the river, the ducks are chattering and the wind casts ripples on the surface of the water. For a moment I stop and watch the sun set the ripples alight, feeling a flicker of something. Then a siren sounds, wailing from one of the roads hidden close by. I spot plastic bottles in the stream and rubbish in the reeds. I keep walking.

As with many days like this, I have no real destination. I work and write from home: there's no need for me to gather myself to reach a fixed point for a certain time. It's a modern life – there's freedom and confinement – an everyday loneliness and the struggle to get going. Feelings that must be echoed in many hearts across the city. The challenge today, as with many days on this stretch, is to walk myself into another headspace.

I like to roam. It's central to my writing. There's something about walking that mirrors the pace of thought. I like the way walking lets me dip in and out of myself – taking notice of the things around me, observing, reflecting and internalising – without getting stuck. I can get lost in thought while my feet keep moving. Walking and thinking, one thing always leads to another.

As a writer, walks can be a vital source of stimulation and inspiration. I'm often in the mountains and those are the places that set fire to my heart. I'm used to working hard to gain eagle-like perspectives. I'm used to covering vast distances and challenging my body to perform. Rock climbing or crossing glaciers, I'm used to moving through landscapes that require my utmost attention. These are places where my senses are keyed – my body working like an instrument in a state of fine attunement, with careful hand and footwork essential. There's focus and challenge but that's not all: I like getting into a space where I feel free, where I can listen to nature, tuning into the living world and everything happening there.

But I live in the city, in one of the most densely populated areas of Scotland. This is where I live, and this is where I write. The challenge in this everyday place is different. Down here, in this busy urban environment, immersed in the stuff of daily life, the problem is how to move the mind? How to enter the right headspace?

Keep moving upstream, past the new-build flats, over the sandstone bridge with the blockwork etchings from deep desert time, up the pavement beside the hawthorns and sycamore, keeping the body moving beside the river enclosed in its canal.

One foot in front of the other, still feeling slow and heavy, tired and lethargic. Today I feel deeply uninspired.

I don't know what I'm looking for. Kicking my feet, I dream of a better elsewhere. Somewhere less urban, less built-up, a place where my eye can soar for miles, taking in vast views. Visions of forests, mountains, fields and glaciers float before me.

Enough, discipline says. I keep walking, trying to ground myself in my feet on the pavement, now. Be here, now, I tell myself. Be here now, with my body, in all its unpleasant unease.

The purpose for today is to release my body. I'm hoping that, simply by moving, I'll shake off my lethargy and open into another state. One foot in front of the other, I'm hoping the gentle magic of movement will walk life into my body and release me into the state of flow. Keep walking, keep looking.

Caminante, wrote Antonio Machado, *no hay camino, se hace camino al andar.* Walker, there is no path, you make the path by walking.

Cross another road, down the steps, and there's a man in the river. A naked man, still as a heron, standing up to his shins in the water, his flaccid penis exposed. Industrial-pastoral, he's made of cast iron, part of the river, with lichens and algae greening the torso, as he stands between the willows and wild roses.

His naked stillness invites me to stop. Eyes closed, the sculpture's face is lifted in a pose that suggests attentiveness. Is he listening? Or seeing something?

Funny how his stillness catches me, as I set out to move but am held now by this fixed point. I watch the water and willows flowing past this moment – this still point in the busy city.

On other days and moods, the sculpture catches me differently. Sometimes I find it creepy, sometimes funny. Sometimes, it seems an act of sublime egotism, the artist recreating himself hundreds of times across this island nation. But today, as I mooch around, hunting for something, the sculpture feels helpful.

Pausing to contemplate him for a moment, I see a window on something different. Another humanity: the human figure, stripped back to a poised form; a person without our restless unease – a person immersed in the river, exposed to the ebb and flow of the seasons.

Then a butterfly lands on a rose and I move on, stepping over a snail in its shell, travelling in the opposite direction.

Following the green artery, my mind still feels weary and distracted; my senses still tired and dulled. This is not the state of mind for making and creating – and yet that is what I seek to do.

In this grey state, I follow the path through the city, emerging onto a busy road, crossing it, and then descending onto the continuation of the old railway line. The road was a sensory onslaught and now, down here, I start to appreciate this path for what it is. A green corridor, dank and organic, away from the road, the noise of traffic and the stress of speed. A breathing space. Brambles and ivy tumble over the walls and trees grow where they can. Nothing is overly gardened or tended; there's an organic wildness that can be hard to find elsewhere in the city.

Why start the day with a walk, I wonder, as I move up the corridor. Why not take the easy path, roll out of bed, go to the desk, and start to make? Sometimes that's all it takes. Some days I wake, my head fizzing with ideas, and the words tumble out. But it is not always so. I often need something else, some kind of stimulation or provocation to bring it out, whatever *it* is, to edge the ideas from formlessness into form. The work is relational.

Here's where the internet might come in, I muse. Living in this moment, I have access to the ultimate source. At my fingertips lies a universe of words and ideas, images and film, people to talk to, conversations to observe or participate in. I can go on epic journeys without ever leaving my flat. I can be challenged, confronted, aroused, devastated – all from my bed or sofa, these various sensations delivered up from a machine in my hand. It is enchanting, intoxicating, encompassing and yet, something is missing.

The walk, I think, has a different nature. It does not hit my brain in the same way that the internet does, with nuggets of information that bounce around my synapses like balls fired into a pinball machine. It's less clear where this wandering is leading. Perhaps it is going nowhere. Perhaps it's an excuse, a work-avoidance strategy.

No, I tell myself as I continue walking away from my desk. It's an unfolding, it's different every time. A walk is full of questions and possibilities, it's a way to enter a loose state of meandering flow. This idea comes to me at a bend in the river and I see the two processes working together: my psyche unconsciously mirroring the forms my feet are following. Something is changing.

Here's dappled light on the cobbles, a grandmother pushing a pram, and the chorus of water tumbling down the rocks in the weir. Beside the millpond I notice, as if for the first time, a brick chimney. I've passed the chimney many times, but this is the time that I notice it, and I wonder, what was here before? Who worked here? How many people were active on this ground once upon a time? What industrial past, what stories and secrets are hidden, buried under the ivy?

Picking up pace, I pass the cherry trees and dog walkers, cross the field, pass another iron riverman. Further up I watch the river weeds, water crowfoot, streaming out in long green tresses, waving and flowing in the clear water. A vision of Millais' *Ophelia* drifts through my wandering eye.

The walk is bringing questions now, and I feel like it's leading me somewhere, as though this walk is taking on a life of its own.

Leaving the river behind, a force draws me onwards, a new spirit, a hint of rebellion awakening now with a touch of desire that sets my feet moving faster along the pavement, through the birch trees that line the cemetery walls, branching right, along the road with views to the castle, across the street, towards the garden.

The garden? Yes, the garden. Pausing at the gates, I feel a twinge of guilt. A rival discipline intrudes.

Stop, it says. Turn around; go home. It's time to focus, to create, the voice says.

I should be at the desk by now. I should be setting words on the page. But the wind is rustling through the leaves and the sun is playing games with light and shadow. Perhaps there's something in here for me – something that will answer the need within – something that will wake me up, shift the haze, and set things moving.

My place, my place, my place, the birds call, singing from the pines.

And so my feet lead on into the garden, following the stream of seeds that floats in the breeze, light as feathers.

And there's *Gloria*, Barbara Hepworth's sculpture in bronze. I cross the grass to come in close and look at what she made. Two diamond forms standing upright, one on top of the other to make a single abstract figure. The surface, both rough and smooth, is textured with a raised bumpy roughness that becomes smooth with the bronze. My hands run over it and I can sense the maker. There's a softness to the form – something both tender and firm – her physicality written into the work. I picture the artist standing here, where I am, hammer and chisel in hand, working the mould. How did she learn to make like this? And how did she come to see like this – to translate the vision from the mind into the form?

Looking through the hole, I see the garden on the other side. Some view this piece as representing hands raised in prayer; others see an intimate female form. I like the open, undefined nature of this piece, gesturing at what may be the mother of human creation but equally could be something else entirely.

I leave these shapes behind and let the walk continue.

Onwards, past *Gloria*, and further into the garden, below a chestnut susurrating, and now on through the cherries and birches and rhododendrons and, in this place, I feel my senses starting to warm up and loosen.

It's just a short walk to get here, but already I feel elsewhere, out of the tired old urban familiar. Immersed among so many plants and insects and species and things I don't know, I can't name, I don't understand, and yet in the presence of all of this unknown, I'm not overwhelmed. I feel my body is waking up; my animal-humanity is coming to life in the presence of all these other living things.

In *The Living Mountain*, Nan Shepherd meditates on how the Cairngorm mountains offer a place where 'may be lived a life of the senses so pure, so untouched by any mode of apprehension but their own, that the body may be said to think'. I find it hard, in the city, with the distractions, the built environment and preoccupations of daily life, to reach this state of exquisite, sensory being; a state that feeds mind and body and stimulates the most generative creative processes. It's hard, but not impossible.

Writing is thinking, thinking is being, and sensory perception is integral to all. The act of walking feels like the thread that runs through these different states, enabling them to open out, like flowers.

There's so much life in here, I think, as I walk through the garden, past holly and oak and Kazakh pear with fruit now growing where the sweetest blossom came this spring. Drifting on through the thousands of plant species I do not know, passing visitors speaking languages I don't know, roaming thus, I start to feel lost, intoxicated, swept away and absorbed inside so many different visions and versions of existence.

Questions bubble up, moving my lips, my tongue. There's a gardener singing on the job, a circular table built around a tree, trees growing at angles that the wind must have once forced them into, and here, just a mile and a half from home, I come to realise that the walk is working.

I left home feeling lifeless, hoping that the simple act of moving my feet would somehow transport me. And it has. I'm inside that place now where stimulation, concentration, focus and interaction are all flowing together. There's life in my limbs, things are breathing and flowing, new pathways opening within. I've moved my feet and moved my mind. But the walk is not over yet. The fire has been lit and there is more to explore.

On the side of Inverleith House – a grand Georgian mansion at the centre of the garden – a giant set of red lips with beautiful white teeth is hanging at an angle, grinning down on the garden. My feet propel me towards this provocation, curiosity grabbing me by the navel, drawing me up the steps and into the old mansion.

Inside, my footsteps echo slightly off the wooden floorboards. The gallery is quiet this morning.

I'd not heard of the artist, but I'm instantly mesmerised by the work. Here's image after image, of men and women, but mostly women, photographs and pictures cut out from fashion magazines, consumer catalogues and pornography. The pictures have been layered up and transformed, grotesquely cut and pasted and engineered into peculiar new forms.

Big lips and strange eyes glued onto glamour models. Flowers pasted over the lips or eyes or breasts or brain.

A couple stand together in a posed romantic scene: he has his arms around her, in an image of intense possession, but the artist has given the woman a fork and new eyes. The woman has jammed the fork into her eyeballs.

The artist is Linder, a punk feminist now in her seventies. The work feels out of place in here – I'm shocked, surprised, delighted that this artist is given this space to turn things on their head. Through a lifetime's collecting and refiguring of soft porn, she has held up her own lens, subverting the male gaze, restoring a peculiar agency to the female objects.

I keep walking, spiralling up the staircase, through one room to another, absorbed, challenged and bemused by these visions before me, looking at picture after picture, Linder's artwork working at something inside me, stirring something, connecting with some question, some thought I had, that I'm carrying with me. What does it all mean? I wonder. How does this connect with the problem I set out with today?

And then I find it. The key that unlocks this peculiar journey.

There's an image displayed in a lightbox. A black-and-white photograph of a woman kneeling on some railway tracks. She's naked, under the trees, on her knees in nature with her hands raised, palms beside her cheeks and ears, fingers tensed, eyes shut, mouth gaping open in an exaggerated expression, a shout, a moan of ecstasy.

The picture is absurd. There's no explanation of where it came from or who the model is, but the artist has done her thing, and brought the twist that explodes the image.

Linder has stuck an enormous coloured flower over the top of the naked woman. The model's breasts and vagina are covered up by this giant lily head in vivid orange and green and white, a flower that's bursting with petals, stamens and carpel, as vivacious as the woman underneath, the flower with all its sex organs displayed in a violent explosion of colour and life and sensuality.

The label on the wall tells me the image is called *The Goddess Who Lives in the Mind.* And there, with the title, and the image, everything starts working together as one, the glamour model on the train tracks given her agency with this title and the erotically charged flower, and suddenly, there is the shock to the mind. Yes.

Yes, I think.

Yes, that's it, I think, as little explosions fire inside my head, through my synapses, and I move on, walking back down the spiral staircase, out of the mansion, and back out through the garden. That's it, I keep thinking as I keep walking, heading back, agitated, past *Gloria*, still holding the thought, letting it come together, journeying home along the path. Animated by my pace, the thought keeps moving, taking shape, drawing in all the little trails and traces from this morning's walk, the nebulous fragments and strands from the Water of Leith now knitting together into something with a clear shape.

That's it, I think to myself as I race back to my desk along the old railway line by the river, with the image of the lily and the goddess on the train tracks strong in my mind, bringing a radiant light to everything I pass. The colours appear more intense, the world more vivid and animated. That's who I set out to meet today, I think. That's who I set out to meet today and every day on walks like this, when I head out of my front door and pace up or down the Water of Leith.

Whether I'm tired and lethargic, or energised and motivated, I walk. I walk to pay attention and find things to notice. I walk to move my body and set things in motion. I walk to connect with my senses and the world around me. But more than this. The walk runs deeper still. The act of walking moves me through the world, and in so doing, it unlocks something. Something fundamental that lives both inside and outside and seems to play somewhere in between the two.

A thing that is a source of energy and vitality. It's the seed, a well, a river – it's a source of inspiration and connection. It's something that is accessible to everyone, everywhere, I think to myself as I pass the Leithers on the benches, the cyclists and pram-pushers. It's the divinity that lies inside us all. The divinity of consciousness. I walk to meet the goddess who lives in the mind.

A Shopping Holiday

Linda Cracknell

The Sunday I left home on my shopping trip, I carried a rucksack with overnight things, adding some Lebanese snacks from the monthly summer market as I passed. Although the A827 still channelled vehicles across Aberfeldy town square where it's held, parked cars were excluded for a few hours in favour of colourfully striped stalls and people ambling between them with baskets over their arms. As with the Greek 'agora', this crucible held a lively and sociable event, bringing in folk from the far west of Glen Lyon or down from hill farms to exchange goods and news. Here were Balhomais Farm vegetables, organics from Little Trochry, cheeses and Nepali snacks. I began my walk buoyed up by friendly encounters with neighbours and traders.

I was on my way to buy a household item in Perth. I wouldn't find it at this local market or in any of the shops near to home. I could have bought it online with delivery included, but before making a choice I needed to handle a few alternatives. I barely admitted to my delight in finding a pretext for a walk, but it felt not dissimilar to the 'need' to buy a pencil that took Virginia Woolf on a glorious evening traverse of London's streets which she justified as necessity and transformed into the beautiful essay 'Street Haunting'.

As a writer I recognised the drive of restlessness and the need for discovery, the resulting excavation of a different version of the self which brought me into step with Woolf. I was also looking forward to the rhythm, the meshing of inner and outer worlds that comes on a long walk; the paring back of the self to something essentially human with the tick-tock motion of my legs. My journey would also be a chance to link up my known ways with some new ones and to lay steps over ways through the land that pre-date vehicular passage.

I've lived in Aberfeldy, thirty miles north-west of Perth, for thirty years, but rarely go to the 'Fair City'. My nearest hospital is there. It has one of three railway stations I might use. But I haven't ever really come to know Scotland's ancient royal capital even though it is linked to my home by the River Tay. These days the Stone of Destiny is housed in a brand-new museum. Apart from this, Perth city centre, like many others, seems a black hole of boarded-up shops bearing 'To Let' signs, while the peripheral retail parks sprawl outwards in glass and steel and concrete.

I don't go there to shop as a rule. My local shops and modest supermarket fulfil most needs, and for many years I've been part of a wholefood cooperative collectively making bulk purchases. Everything else comes from the thrift shop, or I order online when necessary. I don't enjoy shopping as an activity or like the increasing commerciality we seem to live amidst, and it never occurs to me to get in a car to go shopping thirty miles away. But then I don't have a large family and, by deliberate choice, I haven't owned a car for several years.

To find out what persuades my neighbours to drive to Perth's shops I'd raised the question in our local Facebook group. The main purposes by far were, firstly, supermarket shopping and, secondly, clothing. After that came building materials and fuel. While some of these needs can be met back at home, many respondents said it was much cheaper in Perth and there was greater choice.

In preparation for the trip I spread my 1:50,000 Ordnance Survey map (sheet 52) across the floor – coverless, tattered and torn from a great deal of use – and scanned it diagonally from top left to bottom right, Aberfeldy to Perth. Two tracts of land, each roughly square, butt onto each other: one north, one south. Each is bordered by A roads and contains hill land rising above Rivers Tay and Braan to a modest 500 metres or so, unremarkable peaks largely unvisited by comparison with the next ranges north or west, which reach Munro height. No roads cross the more northerly of the squares, and it's not until a few miles out of Perth, in the southerly square, that minor roads begin to lace together small villages around Glen Almond.

By making that diagonal traverse on foot, I'd leave Highland for Lowland, sparsely populated places for city density. I'd make a virtue out of necessity, a 'holiday' out of a deadly dull shopping trip, and I'd stride my local hills with real purpose. Woolf, shedding her indoor home-self to feel gloriously alive, found herself part of a rambling stream of humanity, her eye revelling in surface and light and colour which finally drew her, imaginatively, into the lives of others. But on the route I would be taking, I didn't expect to meet many folk.

Although initially I was on my home territory, I wasn't cavalier about finding the way. I walked with the paper OS map knowing that if later I felt unsure exactly where I was, I could also use my phone to refer to 'OS Locate'. But in order to expand my historic awareness, I'd also spent several evenings scanning the OS map of 1888 using the georeferenced maps viewer from the National Library of Scotland. This service has long informed my walks in Scotland by demonstrating past routes. When layering my footfall over the tracks of past walkers, I feel part of a continuity of people and place. It both feeds my sense of 'home' and, by connecting me to earlier lives, makes me more imaginatively nimble.

Just out of town I took a track rising south from the Tay towards Loch Kennard. I'd cycled it recently with a friend, heading for a swim on a steamy June evening. That's how I knew that I would begin with four miles uphill on a forestry track. It presents a dull proposition, as Sitka spruce commercial monoculture keeps a walker enclosed and obscures the lay of the land. But on that evening, cycling had seemed too fast. Where clear-fell permitted, I'd have liked to seek out views upstream along the Tay Valley, back towards the cloud-topped Munros around Loch Tay or to note branches off the track – potential destinations for another time. I'd needed instead to focus on the rubbly track a few feet ahead in order to keep up cycling momentum.

Walking pace now allowed me to stop and explore the stone-built barn an hour out of the town and elevated at about 300 metres. A house had also stood here once, according to the old OS map. Over the years I've noticed how often relics of crofting townships and farmhouses in this valley sit at about this elevation. High pastures once, perhaps, and views that roll down to the River Tay, or did before the plantations came.

The track was edged with plants quick to colonise land after disturbance: rosebay willowherb, broom, buddleia, birch and cow parsley in great creamy flower heads. Banks of wild raspberry canes trembled with fruit and flies, the air heavy with pollen. By contrast, acres of clear-fell took on an apocalyptic, wartime look: greyish, brash-strewn ground, as if a fire had raged through here. 'KEEP OFF THE LOG STACKS' Euroforest demanded in bold signage, reminding me that I was traversing one of the most commodified parcels of upland in Scotland.

In 1980 the Midland Bank Pension Fund purchased an extensive area of 'derelict grouse moor' (4171.5 hectares) and created Griffin Forest, aiming to maximise commercial timber production, mainly with Sitka spruce. Later it was sold to an individual. At the time it was the largest single-ownership private commercial forest in Europe. In a second wave of opportunism in 2012, one of the largest wind farms in the UK was commissioned here. A significant portion of the thirty-year-old Sitka forest was clear-felled in order to make way for sixty-eight turbines with a 156.4 megawatt capacity, capable of providing electricity to 114,000 homes. Further access tracks and bridges were built, concrete was laid, and giant towers and blades erected. This development was not without significant opposition at the time.

As I write, the entire area of forest and wind farm, now expanded, has been sold for £145 million, achieving a further superlative: one of the most expensive rural estate acquisitions ever made. Walking in this highly commodified landscape, it was hard to think of its centuries and millennia in very different circumstances, but I still hoped that later the land would tell more of its earlier story to me.

An hour further on, approaching Loch Kennard just after the highest point of my walk at 500 metres, a piece of that story appeared: a boarded-up cottage materialising through the dense, dark forest. A sign on it warned of 'danger of death', and a wolf in grandmother's clothing suggested itself. But it was simply a remnant from the days of Loch Kennard Lodge, with its kennels and boathouse marked on the old OS map, used by wealthy fishing and shooting parties from 1870, and later demolished for Griffin Forest.

An old photograph shows a colonial-style building with a wide first-floor balcony overlooking the water and wisps of smoke billowing from a central chimney of three. A rowing boat is pulled up on the shore. A maharajah had stayed there, and a French count who was persuaded to contribute to the erection of the Black Watch monument in Aberfeldy. It had a billiard room, smoking rooms, a hall, numerous bedrooms and staff accommodation. Secrets may be laid here, contracts forged among men, pacts now forgotten or sunk among the reeds.

This day I saw no trace. Loch Kennard, probably from the Gaelic *Cein* – 'still water' – and *Aird* – 'the height': the high, still water whose edge I now walked all alone at 400 metres.

Who, I wondered, might have made a journey such as mine a century or more ago? Perhaps there were commercial imperatives, someone seeking work in Perth's textile industries – linen, cotton spinning, weaving and bleaching, or silk dying at Pullar's. Or a walker might have been carrying produce – cheese or bales of tweed – to the twice-weekly markets, perhaps leading a pony in hand. I'd noticed ways on the old map were regularly marked with the word 'trough', presumably for the watering of travelling animals.

Or maybe a reader wished to borrow or return a book from Innerpeffray – Scotland's first free public lending library – twenty miles south of here, near Crieff? We know, for example, that on a Monday in December 1817 a Pat McFarlen travelled the eleven miles each way from Comrie to the library to borrow Thomas Wildman's *A Treatise on the Management of Bees*. If he used his feet to get there, it's the kind of walking as transport we learn about from Thomas Hardy or Neil Gunn or Jessie Kesson, and which now seems lost to us, despite being a basic capability of many human beings.

Perhaps in the right conditions such a journey might have been pleasurable rather than gruelling. Alexandra Stewart, who was born in 1896 in Glen Lyon, west of Aberfeldy, wrote *Daughters of the Glen*, a memoir of her childhood and growing up there. Although her father was a shoemaker, she wrote about the pleasure of walking the three miles to school barefoot from late spring to early autumn on a soft, dusty surface, kind to the soles of the feet. So much did she enjoy this feeling that she and her sisters would hide their boots in a hole in a wall and collect them again on the way home.

Stewart's father regularly walked the eleven miles into Aberfeldy and then back again in a day. He once walked twenty-eight miles to Glen Almond, just south of the Highland Boundary Faultline, on a route not far west of my own. He walked back the next day, leading a white cow acquired from his cousin.

Stewart observed how an emphasis on speed takes something out of life, as when animals were replaced with engines. An old ploughman claimed he didn't know what loneliness was until he was put on a tractor rather than being in the company of a horse. Most tellingly, Stewart wrote of the value of having 'a well-stocked mind' as its own good company. Long hours spent walking were not a waste of time, she felt, especially when the land was alive with lore and legend as well as, at that time, with people. Some of today's ruins would have been new buildings at the time of her father's long walk.

I've often noted the joys of walking alone and how the meshing of rhythm, thought and observation induces a playfulness of mind which can be creative about land, and can animate evidence of the past. On this Perthshire journey I felt in tune with Stewart – certain that in fine weather, when the local hills could be properly appreciated, such a necessary walk might feel like freedom, just as Woolf found a miraculous renewal in her roaming of London's streets.

On the ways through these hills, greetings and news could be exchanged when other walkers' eyes were met – a reminder of the joys of humanity as well as the capacities of our own bodies and the qualities of the world we move through. Are we too quick in our own age to interpret roads and vehicles as indicators of 'civilised' life?

Given the current climate crisis, but even ignoring that, the priority and space we give to the private car can seem absurdly self-defeating. We barely notice that this symbol of mobility dominates most urban streets. Seen from the air, rows and rows of abandoned cars surrounding a major airport can shock with a visual wake-up call. In the United Kingdom we also seem content to reverse the 'give-way hierarchy' of the sea, where power gives way to sail, the driven to the self-propelled. Take that position as a pedestrian or cyclist and the vocal abuse, at best, keeps us in our 'place'.

Statistics suggest that shopping is the most common reason for car use. In 2020, recognising domestic transport as the highest source of emissions, the Scottish government set a target to reduce by 20 per cent the distance driven in cars by 2030. But in April 2025 they decided it was unrealistic and dropped the target. The one-quarter of households in Scotland who do not have access to at least one car correlate to the lowest incomes. I wonder whether there is a different quality of human relationships in communities where collective forms of transport, or walking, are more dominant.

My last car suffered a ridiculously spun-out and expensive demise which coincided with me acquiring my free bus pass at the age of sixty. Together they provided a major incentive to live without owning a vehicle, and although I live in a rural area without the best of public transport services, it feels critical at this point in history to reduce my personal carbon footprint, even if sometimes it is inconvenient. I travel less as a result, more deliberately, and seek more cooperative, communal ways of travelling (as well as using an e-bike). I've found that a greater degree of planning and consciousness suits me. It takes longer. But I do not stay put. I make journeys by bus or bicycle or by finding people with extra room in their car going to one of the nearest train stations. Sometimes I hitchhike. Walking often makes up the gaps.

In an unintegrated transport system, there are, inevitably, pauses. These can be irritating, but sometimes feel like a luxury when I allow in a different attitude to time. Always there is a book to be read, a notebook to scratch in, something to look at or people to chat to. My years without a car have been rich in encounter, with friendships struck up in a shared waiting room. An opportunity to observe human behaviour is vital to a writer, and I always recommend public transport to new writers looking for ideas. When problems arise and journeys are frustrated, the kindness of others is often life-affirming.

Making an entire journey to Perth on foot may be extreme as a form of transport, but I'm not the only one walking such journeys. Since 2020 the Slow Ways movement has been charting the means to walk between any town, city and national landscape in Britain. I'd consulted their contributors' suggestions for the route from Aberfeldy to Perth, which broadly confirmed my own plan. I also enjoyed the absurdity of telling people in the market square that I was walking to Perth to go shopping. Such a simple, symbolic act may resonate in an age when we look, helplessly, to AI or Fusion or other new technologies to solve our approaching climate catastrophe. It might remind us how the majority world lives: Ethiopia's 10 cars per 1,000 people to the UK's 603 (and New Zealand's 939), or humble us to reconsider the travel methods of our predecessors.

Reading about life in the Aberfeldy area in the early nineteenth century, from John Kennedy's *Old Highland Days*, makes clear that although carts were available for some travel, many miles were covered on foot. This might include fifteen or twenty miles on a Sunday to 'sit under' a charismatic preacher, even though it meant starting at four in the morning and returning home at midnight. Some may have taken up hillwalking to reach illicit stills, or to 'put up' game birds for a party of gentlemen. When Kennedy heard from Loch Tayside that his mother in Aberfeldy was ill, he walked the fifteen miles back in snowdrifts so deep he found himself walking on top of the stone dykes that bounded the fields. My own low-carbon journey to Perth nodded to this rich history, but also gestured to a contemporary urgency – as well as justifying two days of freedom in the local hills.

After Loch Kennard I thought the way would be new to me. I perched on a rock to eat a sandwich, greeting as they passed in straggles a puffing but cheery group of women walkers. Looking east, I realised that the descending track, with its view towards grand open hills flanked by widely spaced wind-turbine towers, was familiar. On a brilliant winter's morning after heavy snow, my friend Kathy and I had traversed it on skis, circling back around a smaller loch as well as Kennard, which, frozen to stone slab and powdered with snow, we had considered skiing directly across.

The 1888 OS map makes clear that, back then, no footpaths completely crossed this massif to join the Tay Valley in a continuous, diagonal route to Strath Braan. The bravest paths from both north and south sides stalled at about 380 metres and left the more elevated hill between to the springs and bogs. These days, the hostile heights can be traversed due to tracks laid for the forestry plantation and wind farm, establishing a reliable through-route for walkers and cyclists between Aberfeldy and Dunkeld, avoiding A roads.

I gently descended the flank of Ben Salachil on a track leading towards Strath Braan under those 124-metre-high turbines. As I strode out, I was entertained by their chorus, an otherworldly, rhythmic whoosh and clunk, whoosh and clunk, mixed randomly with whines, whistling and a dull underground knocking like the sound of a distant, ghostly train on its tracks. An eerie accompaniment. I wondered how people resident a century or so ago on the slopes below might have interpreted such sounds, had they been able to hear them. What gods or sprites might have been conjured?

The views entertained me, too, on this new-to-me southerly track. Further, distant turbines were sited on crag-tops as if making giant stepping-stones of them, visually dramatic against the round, dark hills of Glen Quaich to the west. Beyond Strath Braan, tomorrow's low hills south towards Perth now revealed themselves. I relished this confirmation of a further day's walking which would suspend again my everyday life and its perceived burdens. It was the same 'permission' Woolf sought when she reached a view of the wide, peaceful Thames, to stop and simply enjoy it – seeking a version of herself that had no care in the world.

I knew that the sturdy track I was on is used these days, particularly by cyclists, to drop into the eastern end of Strath Braan and so reach Dunkeld. But the old OS map had suggested a variation to me further west. It would hold me to my diagonal course, a direct line of least resistance towards the village of Trochry, where I would spend one night. This alternative path felt a privilege and made of me an explorer; a way hidden to most but offering me the opportunity to adventure beyond what is generally known of these lands today.

So I left the security of the track and broke out across the slopes of high, rough fields that dropped towards a valley. I used instinct and a compass to discern the old way to a landmark ruined house in a small crease in the hillside: Salachil. Roofless, with mottled grey stone bright against rough grasslands, its door and window lintels were surprisingly intact, suggesting a once-substantial home. Former rooms were crammed with waist-high nettles. Its suggested grandeur, its whiff of Wuthering Heights stilled me to sit with a sandwich. Then I walked the yet-visible outline of a former lane which took me down to a natural terrace at 300 metres on a steep rise above the Ballinloan Burn. Ravens croaked from above and sheep complained at my intrusion among the tumbled walls of this former settlement.

The old geography shared its joys.

An archaeological survey here had found scattered cairns from rock-clearing, strip fields, homesteads, kilns, huts and diverse field systems; a settlement that spanned a prehistoric origin to post-improvement times. This included 'Pitcarmick-type' buildings (stone and timber longhouses of the late first millennium CE). What I found was the sweet sound of a shushing burn below me, meadows knee-deep in buttercups, my head in a sphere of insect buzz and buzzard call. The cry of sheep. It was plain to me that, at least in summer, this would have been a very pleasant place to live. Why would a group of people *not* choose this place, at least to spend summer shieling-time, as clearly happened in some periods.

The sense of a past community remained in the imagined scent of wood or peat smoke. I caught at the voices of children playing, running errands. There was hammering. The cutting of grass for hay. A pastoral, grubby life out of doors, just as I often long for.

On the skyline strode Griffin's towers, haunting the past with their modernity. I enjoyed this juxtaposition. I'd found my way from that 'wasteland' of high bogs and moor turned to industry, the dense uniformity of plantation, the spacious dance of the turbines. And then descended into these pastoral relics and a sense of nurture.

The evening light was already golden when I left the old village to follow the Ballinloan Burn down through deciduous woodland and low, lush fields. I half-expected to meet, coming the other way, a traveller returning to the village, bringing provisions or goods along this ghost track of former times.

I'd never seen these places before, or known of them despite the many hundred times I must have passed through Strath Braan on the tarmac. It struck me how conditioned we are to orientate ourselves and to read the land through what is visible from the road corridors cutting through it.

Exploring on foot has always been my means of affirming myself in a new place, of making it feel 'known' or even like 'home'. Seeing the same hill or ancient tree or building from many angles means I begin to place myself securely within it; trust the 'lay of the land' imaginatively or with my body in motion. Interpreting only from a car window greatly limits this. I was heartened to have finally drawn a line with my feet between Tay and Braan.

*

It was strange to stay in a B&B less than a thirty-minute drive from home, and strange, too, to be surrounded by the trappings of modest luxury after my encounter with the pared-back lives of the villagers of Salachil. But it gave the next morning's start, and the whole walk, a greater sense of continuity as I took the old military road from Trochry east along Strath Braan to cross the arched Rumbling Bridge. Below it the river carves a deep gorge through rock before carrying white water towards Birnam. I leant over the balustrade to glimpse black depths and a glint of spray through laced alder branches: the final assertion of the river's rapids before it empties into the Tay at the Highland Boundary Faultline.

Rather than follow it, I crossed the A road, turning south on a delightful section of old way that I'd walked before. It raised me well above the River Tay's turns in the wooded valley a mile to the east. A clear, straight, sunlit path between two rickles of white stone soon diminished but was always foot-sure as it rose towards the pass of Glen Garr, visible ahead, cutting deep between Obney Hill on the left and a prominent hillfort at Craig Gibbon on the right. The latter was marked with a clump of trees and an obelisk.

Along the way a Scots pine stood sentinel, chittering with flitting yellow flashes of siskin. The wind was at my back and my thoughts ran. In the warm sunshine, ling purpling among glossy grasses, the path and I eased between gentle hills. It was here I was conscious of enjoying moments of great contentment, even *bliss* of a kind: inner and outer observations in an easy dialogue. A stealthy and unforeseen coup of mind and body. Surely others in the past must also have walked into such happiness in their own pedestrian, though functional, ways. A gaggle of girls, perhaps, singing and telling stories as they carried some small items of their father's joinery over the hill to an uncle at the next farm.

The day's pass was easily reached in its final, tight grip between the two hills. And that was it. I'd crossed the Highland Boundary Faultline and was looking down over quite a different landscape – low-lying fields glossed with waves of barley, gentle slopes lined by potatoes. Small lanes and tracks laid a web across the land, where north of here no roads had ventured at all.

To reach this new land I struggled through chest-high bracken which tore at my bare legs. Not for the first time I wished I was carrying a machete. It was a shame, I thought, that this formerly well-used way might become off-putting to walkers. Before setting off I'd looked at John Adair's map of 1683. In the Tay Valley, Dunkeld and other villages were represented by stylised elevations of buildings, clumps of forest. The River Braan branching west to the village of 'Trochrie' was also marked. But the land between the two which I had just walked was an undefined mess of smudgy dark mountain.

'Here be Dragons' (or bogs) it seemed to say.

By the time of John Thomson's 1827 map, the road I'd just taken past 'Craig Opnie' is clearly marked: a pleasing, curved line of continuity.

In choosing my route, I'd wanted to favour ways with a sense of past footfall but I'd also taken into account my own physical and psychological limits. I wanted it to be as direct overall as possible, but past experience warned me not to risk any pathless, uncharted sections, however 'easy' they might look on the map and however conveniently they appeared to join things up. I also wanted as little tarmac as feasible.

So far, so good, but with ten miles still to go from Upper Obney Farm, I was worried about the amount of tarmac ahead. I was now on a metalled lane which would carry me two and a half miles to the village of Bankfoot.

I hadn't seen a soul all morning except for one cyclist. But soon there were roadside houses. Donkeys. Dogs. Gnomes.

It had become hot. My feet were sore.

At Bankfoot I stopped to rest my feet, sitting at a table outside the Nisa convenience store. Feeling hot and overwhelmed, I first looked inside for something wholesome to eat but found myself attracted only to a packet of Eccles cakes. When I went to pay, to include a machine-made cup of tea, the assistant asked: 'Would you like me to make you a *real* cup of tea?' I accepted joyfully.

'Do you know Five Mile Wood?' I asked her.

This was the next part of my chosen route – a tadpole-shaped block of woodland I'd seen on the map running north to south on the far side of and parallel to the A9, Scotland's major northerly trunk road. The name of the wood seemed enigmatic and strangely English, redolent of Winnie-the-Pooh. But the forest has been there for a long time, appearing as part of a designed landscape on a Roy map of 1747, capping a gentle ridge.

The shop assistant told me how to reach the wood under the A9 and I asked her the origin of the name. It was only a little under two miles long, according to the map, so couldn't be descriptive.

She shrugged. 'Because it's five miles from Perth, I think.'

This cheered me enormously. Five miles I could manage. (It was only later that I read it was named for being five miles from *Dunkeld*.)

As I paced the gentle track through Five Mile Wood, the A9 traffic roared through the trees and I accepted that for the remainder of the journey it would shadow me even when not visible. I recalled the opposition to the proposed wind farm I'd walked through the previous day, which at least was making a positive contribution to cutting the use of fossil fuels. There had been concerns about the visual impact from Strath Braan and elsewhere but also about the noise that would be generated.

The corridor of engine whine I now followed south was far more intrusive than the groans and mutterings I witnessed through Griffin. The A9 is generally accepted as necessary infrastructure, but some oppose its complete dualling for the damaging effect of vehicle emissions, and question the wisdom of encouraging more high-speed car travel.

At the southern end of the wood, I removed my boots for a few minutes' relief, noting nearby the railway line I often travel on north of Perth. I've always enjoyed the growth in understanding of geography that walking brings – the iteration of different tracks, trails and tributaries around a centre which builds orientation. The paths I was following between the A9 and railway line would add to my appreciation of the landscape and my place in it when I next travelled at speed.

'That was where I emerged from the wood,' I would be able to say. 'From where I could see that standing stone in the middle of the field.'

Gritting my teeth, I walked a little west to pound a pragmatic mile of cycle and walking lane immediately beside the A9 itself to reach the village of Luncarty, the 'path' as different as it could be to the gentle way I'd taken through Glen Garr. Four lanes of vans, lorries, cars flashed and thundered south and north: parallel channels of atomised humanity. Travellers with an armoured separation from the world.

Of the private cars heading to Perth, I wondered how many carried people who were, like me, on a shopping trip, and how many were occupied by only one person.

Through Luncarty I found a shady, wooded snicket running behind a housing estate which offered a direct line towards the River Tay where it curves westwards again on its way to Perth. Soon I was on the riverside path with glimpses of blue water through the trees. The new Destiny Bridge soared concrete in an impressive arch towards Scone, diverting traffic from the city centre. Rowing boats were stilled for fishing. I was shortly among tangled verges within a woody, cool corridor. Bird call and river hiss released me to an apparently languorous afternoon in which I was simply a walker suspended in my own space and time. The flow of the river encouraged me onwards in its determined progress towards the sea.

Perth and its traffic, shops, car parks seemed far removed.

But soon I was turning alongside the minor tributary of the Almond River to pass under a rail bridge and then under the A9 again, where kingfishers and goldfinches and pop heroes are painted onto the piles. And then out onto a broad stone bridge around which some teenagers lolled in the afternoon sun. Over the balustrade I watched a heron standing knee-deep in the Almond, cool-footed and hot-headed, apparently oblivious to the traffic rush just over its head. Each of us stood in our parallel universe.

I wasn't sure exactly where I would emerge, but a few more paces delivered me from this traffic-less, woody enclave to a kerb and tarmac next to the Arnold Clark showroom. I could have popped in, there and then, to buy a car for £30,000. But after crossing a rush-hour road, I reached a retail park. Huge store fronts flashed in sunlight; car parks spread around me with no obvious pedestrian ways. Far from the market square from which I'd set out, where John Kennedy said famous storytellers used to congregate to tell of fighting clans and witches and ghosts, the walking human here had little opportunity for interaction with others.

A few more steps and I was at a shop entrance. My reflection in the sliding glass doors – rucksacked, booted, sun-scraped – made of me an incongruous shopper. Nevertheless, I continued on my mission and, after checking out a few different models with the help of some obviously weary assistants, I made my purchase.

From the western window of the bus on the way home, I smiled to see some of my recent landmarks again so soon, especially where Glen Garr dipped through the line of hills above Bankfoot. From now on, this feature, which surely in the past would have signalled a trusted way between the glens on foot, will serve as a motif for my slow journey to the markets of the south. The shopping trip had become an 'escape'; a two-day adventure, freeing mind and body to bring me imaginatively closer to the lives of others.

The spoils I returned with did not include a pencil, as it did for Woolf. I came home instead the proud owner of a new vacuum cleaner.

The Walk as Poem

Helen Mort

Part 1: Lies I tell about writing

South Greenland, 2023. I'm navigating a deserted shore, watched by a dozen icebergs, following a line so faint it must be a desire path, one made by the deviations of others. Among the pebbles is a matte, white rhombus shape. I scoop it up – a little lump of polystyrene from the town dump. When I hold it up to the horizon, it looks like a small imitation of a berg, a model, sad and hopeful. I pocket it and walk on.

As I walk, I'm aware of its presence, the shape it makes in my clothing as I carry it. I take the track towards the old mink farm, now deserted, the far edge of town. That's when words start cleaving to each other, something about the plastic imposter against the strange, majestic forms of ice. The juxtaposition of it. I sense a line of poetry: iambic, regular. I start mouthing the words to myself, silently, glad that I'm not being observed. I walk for an hour to see where it takes me. I will jot nothing down until I get back.

For as long as I can remember, I have been telling people that I write my best poems like this, away from my desk, lines written to the heartbeat and footfall of walking or running. This is true except when it is a lie. Often I don't write like that at all. Often I don't walk like that either. Sometimes I think the extent of the truth depends on where we (or where I) decide writing begins. Is it the form of a piece when it reaches the page or much earlier? Is it the embodied poem, the one held in my mind as I run, repeated silently over and over until some lines 'stick'? Or is it not a poem until I write it down in my notebook afterwards, hands still chill from being outdoors? Or does the poem begin much earlier than all that, with the idea I take for a walk with me, the notion of something I might write? I am wary of any account of the creative writing process becoming self-mythologising.

The first time I can consciously remember this mobile writing practice happening was in the Fens. I was in my early twenties, living in a shared house in Cambridge next to a cemetery. Dusk held a particular kind of melancholy there, the big skies over Mackenzie Road and Mill Road and Parker's Piece, the view into the huge swimming pool and the bodies circling in the water. Bicycles, everywhere. I was always a bit bleary, always going out too late. I used to write letters in those days and I had been reading some post from my old friend Richard in Chesterfield. He'd included a poem from Rainer Maria Rilke which he admired and wanted to share with me. There was a quotation I couldn't shake: 'beauty is nothing but the beginning of terror'. I liked it – I wasn't sure what it meant, but it gave me goosebumps.

I put my phone face down on the desk and stepped out of the house. I took Rilke for a walk with me, round the block. I repeated the line inwardly. When I was about 800 metres from home, I overheard something in my own thoughts. It was a beginning, a springboard, almost like the start of a fairytale:

> *'When Beauty stumbled down my road, knocked*
> *at my door...'*

Once I 'heard' that, I pictured Beauty as a woman, slightly drunk and dishevelled. Someone to be wary of. A kind of terror. I might not have understood Rilke, but I was responding to him. I wanted to know what happened next in the new poem, so I kept walking. When I reached the end of my street, I set off on another loop. I circled round and round, using rhyme to help me 'find' or 'uncover' a narrative, enjoying the surprising choices that kind of sound-based connection-making can force you into. Part of the challenge was to remember the lines without having any way of committing them to writing – which ones were more memorable? Which could I forget and therefore stand to lose?

Once I'd made one poem like this, I found the process somewhat addictive. I experimented with using it to 'solve' other writing conundrums, expand on ideas I thought I had but couldn't articulate in a satisfactory way. Problem? Take it outside. Living in Grasmere in the Lake District for a year from 2010 to 2011, I justified my newfound methodology by drawing on William Wordsworth's practice: he was a walking writer too, composing while on the fells of the northwest of England. I took poems out for walks with me around Rydal Water and over Alcock Tarn. I came to see the poem as something like an errant dog – we might set off in the same direction, leashed together, but then the work would become something, I had to follow and call back, chase through the bracken swearing as it pursued some small prey or disappeared under a lip of rock. A poem is seldom an obedient creature, I found.

When describing this walking methodology, it's easy to simplify it into cause and effect, or a kinetic 'formula' for writing. The experience itself is more complicated, more contradictory, as (perhaps) all embodied experience is. Sometimes I walk in order to write, but more often the genesis of a piece of work is a kind of ambush. At times, I walk to avoid poems, too. Taran N. Khan has written about this aspect of process, saying, 'I walked to be able to escape the page. To get some air, in the widest sense of the word ... When the path through words became obscured, I left my desk and walked.' I find it interesting that here Khan maps a metaphor from walking onto the writing process itself – 'the path through words'. This implies navigation, and a path 'through' surely invites us to take it, see where it leads. Escaping one path (the literary one) by finding another one, a visible and tangible one in our immediate physical environment. The moment when we abandon the idea of committing something to words and pitch our bodies into the world, only to find (sometimes) that this makes the words arrive. Do I do this? Yes.

If this is a kind of avoidance, it is a productive one and it complicates my sense of the relationship between walking and writing. What strikes me when I think back to that Rilke-inflected walk in Cambridge, and the genesis of what would become the poem 'Beauty', is that I was using movement as a kind of distraction: I was finding Rilke difficult, I'd been pushed to the edge of my understanding, provoked to feel complicated. In response, I felt the urge to move. The avoidance of difficulty led to the beginning of a piece of creative work.

No. Start again. That's a half-truth. Once more, there's a mythologising of process going on here as I talk about my writing practice. I haven't told you everything: I didn't just set out that day to avoid the difficulty of Rilke. I was also avoiding the difficulty of emotion. I was sitting with my friend's letter and quotation because I had been in the house all day waiting for a text from a man I was falling (slightly, delicately) in love with. I was hoping he was going to invite me to walk down Mill Road and meet him in our favourite pub, where the back room smelled of smoke and stale lager and lime and the dartboard was perilously close to the heads of the customers. To admit this is embarrassing. His silence was dismaying to me and the hours stretched. For some reason, I always felt I had to wait for him, for his contact, his permission to move, to walk, to initiate, even to write to him. This seems bizarre for someone whose life's vocation has been to make, to create, to set out. Yet there I was, checking for a text that never came. And that propelled me towards Rilke, towards my walk and – ultimately – towards my poem.

So, I've come to think of the poem-walk as a collaboration. An avoidant collaboration, sometimes. If I return to the image of William Wordsworth striding across the fells, solitary and glorious, drafting lines in the rich privacy of his head, I must contrast it with me in Cambridge, pining over a man I'd met in a bar one night, writing a poem on the move to help myself forget about him for a few moments. Am I less literary for this? When I think of the poem 'Beauty', I still think of that man, a little ghost in the margins of the piece. Is this an admission of creative failure? Or did Wordsworth have his own collaborators – his sister Dorothy, the others he surely held in mind? Did Wordsworth have his ghosts too?

If I am to write honestly about writing and walking, I have to demystify my own process, move beyond an image of (to paraphrase and co-opt Kathleen Jamie's notion of the 'lone enraptured male') the 'lone enraptured poet'. Even as I sit here now, writing about process, I realise I have the outline of a 'you' in mind, a projected reader who subtly influences my every move. I can't walk without being haunted.

Part 2: Sometimes a poem is a walk

In 'A Poem is a Walk' (1967), A. R. Ammons argues that the purpose of poetry is to go 'past telling' and towards illuminating 'an existence which can incorporate contradictions, inconsistencies, explanations and counter-explanations and still remain whole, unexhausted and inexhaustible; an existence that comes about by means other than those of description and exposition.' To make the case for a poem being a walk, Ammons defines walks as an externalisation of a kind of 'inward seeking': we have the impulse to go somewhere and so we go. We turn a desire into something embodied, observable. Like a walk, a poem is an embodied phenomenon. This is implicit in Ammons' argument and finds support in the work of poets like Don Paterson, who defines a poem as a 'little machine for remembering itself', a form unique within the literary arts because it can be memorised (I might interject to point out that it rather depends what genre of poetry we are talking about), and carried round within the reader's memory, within their body.

Ammons argues that a poem, like a walk, is unreproducible in the form of original encounter, and suggests that all poems and all walks include the prospect of return. Generally, Ammons says, we end where we started, but not always. These turns and implied returns give shape to the walk or the poem. We set out with a sense of this shape or contour and then we have our intuition verified or disproved. Finally, the motion produced by walking or by the poem is irreproducible, since it is particular to the body of the person enacting it. It cannot be easily translated (or rather paraphrased) in another body. We can only 'know' it by interacting with it ourselves.

If I try to apply A. R. Ammons' theory to my own writing practice, I keep glitching on the problem of the concept of 'the walk' as singular. The walks that I have taken over the course of my life so far are all so different and various that they can barely be classified together.

For example, a walk around Kentmere with my dad when I was small, possibly no older than five or six. Perhaps it isn't a memory at all but a wish or fabrication. The only part of this thirteen-mile undulating route I remember is reaching a track near the end and having to be fed Kendal mint cake as an incentive. I've redone the route since and the track in my memory corresponds to one which leads back towards the starting point, but is that part grafted from those other journeys?

Or the first real walk I did with my toddler after lockdown restrictions lifted in the UK and after he had learnt to move around on two legs. We went to Burbage South and inched our way slowly along the path below the gritstone lip and then back again. The weather was wild, wind plucking at us, and we saw no one.

What about the walk with my grandmother from my silver car to the service-station entrance when she was in her nineties and we were on a road trip north. Is the action of walking enough to make something, anything, a 'walk'? She was never so mobile again. Though it must have been less than a hundred metres, it sticks in my mind like an epic adventure.

Or a stroll to Rydal and round Grasmere lake with my ex, him in unsuitable shoes, stopping at three pubs along the way. I remember passing the pub where Samuel Taylor Coleridge reputedly went for his breakfast and me asking him about what it was like to have a child at eighteen, how he managed. But perhaps we also had that conversation walking in Bridlington or Holderness, an impossibly open landscape.

The walk in Greece where I barely glanced up from the map, the urgency of plotting and following the right route as a woman on my own in blazing sun. Goats with goat bells, parched ground, water pipes, a small white church.

Crossing glaciers in East Greenland, roped to my friends, crevasses gaping on either side. To walk across such terrain requires a special kind of attention and awareness, both of surroundings and of others on the rope. The route is dictated by the formations. Perhaps all walks are, but glacier crossings foreground this. After eight hours of walking in that way, I stopped with my hands on my knees and wept. I think I was crying for the scale of things and our utter insignificance.

Or the walk around Loweswater with my dad one May, being aware – even then – that we might never be this happy again. Him fit and tanned and freckled. I thought then that there would be other times to walk there, but there were not. When I think of it, do I remember the sensations of that sunburnt day, or do I inflict nostalgia upon it, now that my father has had severe strokes and can't walk independently at all? Which version would be truer?

Something I immediately notice from this list is that I privilege the idea of the wild or non-urban walk. Even though some of those prescient memories involve cities, there's a distinctly pastoral bias in my thinking. Does the environment change the walk-as-poem?

If a poem can contain 'contradictions, inconsistencies, explanations and counter-explanations', then so must any account of what it is to write one. It may be as messily embodied as a walk, the business of writing about a subject faithfully. And both walk and poem may implicate others. To return to Khan on walking and writing, there is a democracy in this process we often ignore when we describe writers who walk. As Khan observed in 2025, 'To think of the relationship between walking and writing as something that belongs only to writers is to think of creativity as a form of production, not a way of being. The street teaches you, and the street belongs to everyone.'

I am not alone when I walk, even if I think I am.

Part 3: Sometimes a walk is a poem

Ammons maintains that the walk is particular to the body of the person enacting it but says little about the factors that may influence how those bodies move. I want to test Ammons' theory that a poem is a walk, but I want to do it in reverse. I want to see if a walk can be a poem I make with my body and if the facts of the body change the kind of poem the walk is.

Just now I am in Yerevan, Armenia, at the Yerevan International Book Festival. I have never been here before. It is a landlocked country in the highlands of West Asia, bordered by Turkey to the west, Georgia to the north and Azerbaijan to the east, and Iran and the Azerbaijani exclave Nakhchivan to the south. A world away from my home in South Yorkshire. This affords an ideal opportunity to observe and experience. Can I walk like I write?

I have to start with the facts of the body: I am a cisgendered woman who will turn forty in a few weeks. I am five feet ten and 'medium build'. These descriptors are inadequate and freighted: I can't type anything about my weight or body shape without summoning the ghost of a history of eating disorders, or worrying about what any description of body 'type' might make the reader (particularly the female reader) feel. Even so, I'll persist. The discomfort I feel becomes part of the body which writes and thinks and walks.

I have nothing at present within the composition of my body that affects my ability to cover distances without discomfort, though I don't know what my body will do in future. On a small scale, I have several blisters on my toes and heels from too many laps around the streets near my hotel yesterday in unsuitable sandals: leather with a slight heel. Today, I am wearing flat trainers, a white loose vest top for the late summer heat, and black jeans. I have a hip problem from birth which means that my right hip often clicks loudly as I walk, but nobody else can hear it. I am acutely conscious of it, though, remembering a time when the doctors said I would always have a limp, would never dance or run.

I have dyed blonde hair below my shoulders, a full face of makeup worn for an appearance on stage later – foundation, mascara, dark red lipstick – and several facial piercings: nostrils, septum, philtrum. Most noticeably,

I'm heavily tattooed. In the clothing I'm wearing today the ink that covers both arms is visible, but some of my tattoos are permanently on display anyway: the backs of my hands and fingers, my palms. I have a large outline of a flower winding around my neck and throat, an underchin tattoo and several on my face, including my forehead. The history of each of these designs is complex and can't be known to the casual viewer. What is indisputably obvious is that I am densely illustrated.

I walk awkwardly, a little skittishly. My partner has always described me as moving like a deer stepping into woodland, tentative at first and then more definite. Once, when I was hurrying for a bus in Sheffield, striding purposefully and glancing over my shoulder from time to time, I was stopped by a police car. The officer told me they were concerned that I was being followed because I appeared so nervous, so intensely vigilant. A lifetime of encounters has taught me to map my surroundings, cross the road when necessary, keep my eyes on the floor when I pass a group of men. Are these details important? Are they the walk-poem's background research or are they part of the poem? I think both.

Those are the facts of the body, this body, on this particular morning.

There are also accessories to my walk. I am carrying a tote bag, navy blue with white letters emblazoned across it: *whatever happens poetry survives (Preti Taneja)*. I am also carrying a certain heaviness behind the eyes, the effect of a long plane journey which didn't conclude until 5 am. I am carrying the guilt of leaving my six-year-old son behind at home with his father, who is recovering from illness. I am carrying a deeper guilt that I haven't seen my parents in a while.

Some of this guilt feels particular to walking: my father had a life-altering stroke in 2022 and can no longer walk or move independently. All my memories of learning to love the Peak District and its maps and routes with him as a child are now freighted, overlaid with this knowledge. Each time I walk or run now, I am also overwhelmed with a sense of immense privilege and responsibility. I must do this, I must value this because he cannot. So many of the steps I have taken since he was first hospitalised have been taken in this knowledge. I'm often visited these days by the spectral thought of what it might be like to lose agency over my movements as he has done. I am also, as it happens, carrying the ghost of a line of poetry. It came to me when I was half awake:

> *'Give me a name and I will bring it, budded and*
> *hushed to your feet.'*

I wrote it in my notebook in the night, 3 am, lit by a little table lamp. I couldn't seem to take it any further. I got frustrated with myself. A second thought emerged. Sometimes my mind feels like a well-sealed jam jar and the lid won't give when I try to turn it. I try hot water, greater force. I worry that I need the help of an important and useful man. The line of possible poetry and the jam-jar image become a kind of collage; I shuffle them around like a kaleidoscope. Other thoughts – immediate sensory thoughts – intrude too. I'm hungry. I need a coffee. I'm mildly dehydrated.

The walk begins when I close my hotel room door and take the stairs down to the lobby. Or does it? Does a walk always imply the existence of outside? Everything is quiet except the clanking of the nearby elevator. I push through the glass door of the hotel and the heat slams against me. It is only morning but the sky is holiday swimming-pool blue and the traffic on Argishti Street is already streaming past, horns blaring. I imagine I can smell thyme. Arriving in the night, the city seemed to have a scent of mushrooms, something feral.

If this walk is a poem, when will I find the title? Usually, drafting a piece on the page, it is the last thing to come. In this case, will the destination – a coffee shop on Pushkin Street – become titular, defining? That seems to run counter to Robert Frost's assertion that a poem must reveal, must surprise, for if there is 'no surprise in the writer' there will be 'no surprise in the reader'. Does the title of a poem influence how we read it in the same way that a map guides a walk?

I start up a slight incline. No breeze, just the air full of sound from the churches and the mosque, singing that seems to rumble through everything, emanating from underground. I look for the source and I can't find it. Blossom in the trees, candyfloss-bright. Reddish-brown buildings, Armenian script on the road signs I am too ignorant to read. Bold graffiti.

The road I'm following arcs round, trending rightwards and, when I reach the top of the mild hill, there are more people. Here comes the first interruption and the first problem with mapping poem-as-walk onto walk-as-poem. A man I pass starts shouting something at me. I don't know what he's saying. My heart hammers pathetically. I apologise for my English and walk on, faster, with him still yelling after me. This has happened multiple times in my movements around the city. One elderly man in a khaki t-shirt stood in my path and opened his arms wide as if he was contemplating the prospect of flight. I couldn't work out if it was a rebuke or an invitation to hug. Men have followed me, asked for my number, remarked on my tattoos in English. Someone spat on the street next to me and I wasn't sure what their target was.

In a poem, the pauses come from line breaks and stanza breaks. I often tell students that these are places of emphasis. If there is emphasis today in these interruptions, the emphasis is placed on my female body, my tattooed body.

There is no contemplative peace in the stanza breaks enforced by unwanted attention. There is no silence. My stride is altered by this: the rhythm of my walking poem. My walk becomes a collaboration with everyone who looks at me and speaks to me. I become aware of being unfamiliar with the character of each street, vulnerable to touch. I'm thinking again about how I wrote 'Beauty', how I was collaborating then with a person who probably didn't even know I was holding him in mind.

As I walk, I also remember that I am menstruating. It is the heaviest day of my period and blood is already starting to warm the inside of my leg, leaking onto my jeans. If this was a poem in a creative writing workshop being offered up for critique, I might be telling the author that such visceral details were unnecessary, prurient. The poem might be deemed to have entered the mode of the awkwardly confessional or – seen charitably – what poet Sharon Olds calls the 'apparently personal' ('apparently' because how do we know?). Why is this a detail to include in the poem of the walk? Because I have menstruated on expeditions around the world, as many female bodies do. I have had my period in the mountains of East Greenland and grappled with the problem of what do with sanitary products or how to change them during days moving across the expanse of a glacier. The act of walking is influenced by whether one bleeds or doesn't bleed, whether or not that bleeding is present tense or a premonition, cramps in the stomach, a feeling of bloatedness, irrepressible tears. The experience of menstruating may be as irreproducible as the walk or the poem. Perhaps these embodied aspects that are invisible to others function like the metre or hidden form of the poem: things that subtly structure the verses and influence word choice.

I turn onto a quieter avenue and my pace slows. I am noticing as I walk all the things that make this city different from all the others I have visited before in the world. The men spreading gravel around the bases of trees, each of them using a baby stroller or a pram to store and transport the sacks of stones. The gangs of cats who lounge and prowl and stretch until they're startled by groups of stray dogs who barrel into view and chase them. The greetings traded from window to window across the street. The restaurants with the sprinklers that suddenly puff out a mist to cool customers down. Names of coffee shops. The feeling of shade, brief and welcome and surprising. All these details are the kind of thing I might sprinkle liberally across a poem, expecting the reader to infer significance from each choice. Those aren't just any old cats! They become meaningful within the space of the poem, but on a walk, they are just fact. They are interpreted only by me, as the observer. In a poem, the reader brings their own associations and memories, their own speculation. Is walking an over-signifying enterprise the way a poem is? Is this an aspect Ammons neglected? If a walk is a collaboration and also a kind of poem, I think it's important to consider the aspect of collaboration between writer and reader.

Turning off Pushkin Street and back towards the busier central parks and squares, I realise I haven't a clear sense of when I want to stop. For once, I have no immediate deadline. I am walking in the manner of what Lauren Elkin calls 'Flaneuserie', loitering gloriously in an unfamiliar urban environment, my steps illogically patterned. I am free to sit down on benches or pause under the canopy of a tree or nip into a bar if I want to. But I do not. And how 'free' am I in practice if my physical presence on this walk has attracted attention I didn't want? How is my route determined by factors like gender? I realise that the movements, the shifts my poems make on the page, are governed by the same dance between apparent freedom and implicit constraint: there are sometimes things I do not include, things I do not write about because I anticipate judgement, or because I am bound by the limitations of form.

I am aware that the rhythm of my footsteps should be helping me to organise my thoughts, should be leading that line of poetry from this morning's sleep back into view. It does not come. Instead, there are just entrances with half-glimpsed staircases, glossy shopfronts, doorways to underground rooms, women sweeping dried leaves up from the pavements, stooping with attentive deference to the task.

Just as my walk has no natural end, no 'destination', nor does my writing. This is the point of an essay where it is traditional to say something by way of conclusion, but the connections between poetry and walking still feel overwhelmingly inconclusive to me. They are open to speculation, further testing, revision. If my walk in Yerevan is a poem, it is not one that I am writing all by myself. Walking through an unfamiliar and peopled place is more collaborative, and different bodies have different restrictions placed on their ability to walk freely. My own experience is particular, 'irreproducible' (as Ammons would say). I carry with me all the walks I've done before and the projected idea of all the walks I might take in future. When I try to put this into words, I feel the present being crowded out by those visions from time passed and time as yet unencountered. I exist in the slivers in between: the small but compelling decisive moment of the word, the line, the poem.

On Walking and Not Doing it Right

Kate Davis

Since I became an old woman I've written with enthusiasm and at length about walking, not walking, and the ground under my feet.

For years I generated a knotted mass of poems that never seemed to have any sense of direction; poems that circled back, crossed and recrossed each other. There was nothing to help me work out where, if anywhere, they were going; I could never separate one from another. When I realised in my sixties that the earth I walked was all I ever wrote about, that every poem was trying to find the paths I'd taken, it was a huge surprise.

Some of these poems have been hard to look at close up and most had never made sense to me. They're full of things that might have happened, things I could have made up, things I think I've remembered. Or maybe I dreamt all of them? Now and then I lift up a poem to look for an answer. Often it's an opportunity to hold a piece of the puzzle – how I feel about the ways in which I've tried to move through the world – to consider it from different angles and in a new light. Finding out how my poems capture those movements has been engrossing and revealing, occasionally shocking and, once or twice, thrilling.

By contrast, whenever someone asks me to write about walking, I'm immediately unreasonable, resentful and bad-tempered. This is no exception: I'm annoyed to be asked. It's hard enough doing it, for fuck's sake – now someone wants me to write about why walking matters. My jaws are too tense and there are vertical tramlines down my forehead. I'm a sweary woman and I am swearing.

I caught paralytic polio when I was four and I will loudly and swearily defend my right to cope with my disability in any way I choose, even when – especially when – I know that what I'm doing isn't helping.

From the start I knew my walking was better when I wore callipers and orthopaedic footwear. I knew, too, that if I was braver about allowing people to see my wasted leg, it was possible that its existence would cease to have such an emotional hold over my life.

I refused the callipers and shoes, and knowing that someone was watching me – looking at my leg, my limp – held, and to some degree still holds for me, a horror I find hard to describe. I consider hiding to be a valid coping strategy. I choose cover.

Aside from my natural defiance and stubbornness, I've always had reasons for not doing the things that made sense. The visual evidence of disability, like my thin leg and my limp, make me unacceptable. The things that would help me walk: callipers, orthopaedic footwear, a stick – don't mention sticks – I do not need a fucking stick – are further evidence.

And in terms of my chosen way of coping, well, I suggest that you fuck right off with your empathetic face, particularly if you feel like sharing with me your personal experience of overcoming 'sensitivities' and finding empowerment and self-esteem.

And by the way, don't bother to tell me that being honest about my body is part of healing myself. I hide my leg because it's ugly. I know it's ugly. You know it's ugly. Let's not pretend that when you see it you're not going to feel at least a bit repulsed. I've had seventy years of people's faces and their whispers. When I tried to explain a leg-related problem to a GP at my practice, he clearly didn't know anything about post-polio problems and wasn't interested. I had to show him my leg. He recoiled; he actually took a step back with an appalled look and said, 'I haven't seen anything like that since I left India.'

Even the word *disability* has made me shrivel with shame most of my life. When asked by officials if I had a disability I got angry – I was categorically not disabled, so don't even ask. Disabled kids went to special schools and did handicrafts. They were smiling, brave children for whom people had collecting tins and made charity plastic statues of pretty girls with bows in their hair. Those plastic girls wore pretty dresses, white socks and callipers on their pretty legs. Each girl held a box of her own with a slot in the top where people could pop a few pennies so she could have new callipers, a blue government-issue three-wheeler invalid car and a job at Remploy. How I envied those girls their blonde, ribboned hair and their dresses. How I hated them and their pleading, bright little smiles. I still do.

Now you see how unreasonable and sulky I am about all this.

What was the question?

Actually, I do need a stick. My walking has deteriorated and I'm too old to cope with the joint-shuddering stumbles and bone-thwacking falls. Some trips are spectacular: I fall with a suddenness and clatter that causes onlookers to gasp and cover their mouths. A brief glance up from my feet to check where I'm going can lead to me hitting the floor hard or finding myself pitching forward, head-butting the pavement with a force that makes my brain judder and gives me a headache for the rest of the day. I can walk – I just can't do much of it without stumbling and falling. Even with two sticks I must keep my eyes open and glued to the ground every second. I must keep my wits about me and not allow myself to be distracted. I must be alert to the fact that the smallest change in the angle or level of the ground will require constant gyroscopic mental and physical adjustments to keep me safe. It's relentless but if I don't keep at it there will be injury.

When I started relearning how to walk after my illness I realised the extent to which the ground could not be trusted. Rocks, fields, paths I'd skimmed over without thinking now demanded my complete attention. Tree roots snagged my bad foot. Tussocks of grass sent me sprawling. The pot-holes in the lane unbalanced me. These regular falls made me hyper-conscious about how intrinsically untrustworthy the ground is, even without a lame leg.

Take limestone – I was born and grew up on a limestone landscape. Limestone dissolves in rain; what's left is an empty space you can't see, a lightless cavern growing imperceptibly, creeping towards the surface until there's only a thin layer of turf between it and you. One day the final gram of soil will slip soundlessly sideways, roots will rip asunder, the ground will be gone and you'll be falling into the waiting black earth. There are many ways to fall into the earth; I know all of them.

On top of the perils of limestone, my home on the Furness Peninsula in Cumbria is peppered with old mineshafts, long abandoned and left to fill with icy, red water and bad air. There was one in the next village to where I grew up. No one seemed to have been worried by its existence when they built their new railway to Barrow to haul out the iron ore, but they were reminded at 7 am on Thursday 22 September 1892 when the Barrow to Carnforth goods train stopped at the sidings and driver Thomas Postlethwaite saw cracks opening up in the ground below him. He jumped clear as the earth split open and the train fell into a deep, sheer-sided hole nine metres across. Everyone round our way knew that story. I might have seen a photograph – a stricken face – a man in mid-air – leaping for his life as the earth fell away.

Worse even than abandoned mines are the centuries-old trial bore-holes in fields and woods hereabouts. Less than two metres wide and who knows how deep, commissioned by iron-hungry industrialists and geologists chancing their arm on the long shot, they are left open to the sky like grinning, toothless, waiting gobs.

Under cities and towns across the world are vast networks of old sewers and piping ducts. When they give way there is no time to run to safety. I've seen pictures of cars teetering on the edge of a gash in the ground outside someone's bay window, a street opened up with buildings, traffic, people and streetlights swallowed into a raw wound draped with gushing water pipes and ripped cables. I've watched and rewatched videos of towering trees sinking sideways and sliding under the water of the Florida Everglades.

Sinkholes are my nemesis and my thrill. I call them my geology porn. I dream of them, of falling through the earth, yet I can't resist looking at them. They're not vindictive but they're relentless and they don't suffer fools. They grow like hollow tumours everywhere and that weird, unnatural, frightening hole in the field near my childhood house was definitely one. The village tarn was known to be bottomless. The local legend was of a great hole opening up, filling with water and swallowing the old village down. It's a sinkhole. I know it. I don't need confirmation.

Even before I caught polio I think I understood that the ground was unreliable, deceptive; that the ability to walk across it unmolested is grudgingly granted and easily taken away. Yet most of you appear to believe the earth is solid, dependable, that it'll always hold you up. It isn't and it won't. I don't understand you. Listen – *the ground cannot be trusted.* I need a stick.

One odd exception to the stick rule is that if I'm careful I can dance for a bit without it, and without falling. I've worked out it's because dance means that it's natural, or at least doesn't look weird, to lift my feet up in a way that means I'm less likely to trip over them. This is not, however, a workable technique for walking.

So – to the question – why does walking matter?

I don't know why they're even asking. Obviously walking matters. It's good for us, everyone knows that. Ask the Romantic poets who strode the Lake District in horizontal rain without Gore-Tex, GPS or a thermos. Ask country folk with massive social media profiles and a bestseller under their belt. Ask ramblers, orienteers, explorers of far places and urban adventurers; ask any of them why walking matters and what it could do for us if only we'd give it a go. And doctors – you should definitely ask them. They're very keen to tell you that walking is important and we should do more of it. They're especially keen when they don't appear to be doing much of it themselves. And TV documentary makers, who love to position gorgeous presenters on rocky outcrops, one foot raised on a convenient boulder, chin up, gazing out at a panorama of wonder while a drone circles overhead.

Stop it, all of you.

And to you, the lone enraptured males, and females, demonstrating just how easy it is – stand up/ put one foot in front of the other/ repeat/ bit of a scramble/stand on a rock/ saunter back down feeling and looking fabulous – being out in the landscape is nothing like that for many of us. We know that green places can be soothing, that walking may help anxiety and ease distress, but for some people it is not going to make us better. When you keep going on about it as you waltz along ridges and pose on peaks it makes us feel like shite because we're clearly not doing it right – we are not better. All your inspirational presentations hold within them questions, assumptions, expectations. What we hear is:

How hard can it be?

What are you waiting for?

What's up with you?

What do you mean, you can't?

Have your really tried, though – I mean really?

Are you sure you're not just a lazy bastard?

Have you thought about yoga?

And this – the comment I've brought upon myself by my deliberate hiding of my disability and determination to look normal:

You look all right to me.

Sure, walking matters, of course it does. But walking matters more when you can't do it. Or if, like me, you can't do it properly.

Limping and tripping up isn't doing it properly and you can't hide those things. I don't know if doing it badly is worse than never being able to do it at all, though I doubt it. The periods when I haven't been able to walk have been fairly short and temporary; I can, however, speak from having lived a lifetime of not doing it right.

Imagine walking.

Now imagine not walking.

Your legs have forgotten how to walk. One morning you wake up and they can't do it; they are crumpled underneath you like overripe fruit and you can't make them work.

The virus that got into your body has reached the core of your spine and located a group of your motor neurons. It's burrowing in, replicating itself.

As it multiplies, your neurons are dying.

Now, because they no longer have any motion sensors, your muscles are dying too. There is no cure – they will wither away.

From today you will no longer be able to use that part of your body. It has become a sick snag, a dead thing you must drag around for the rest of your life.

You are no longer normal. You are disabled with all the piercing implications of that word.

It's happening to me but I'm four years old and know nothing about the future. All I know is that I'm sitting in a patch of sunlight on the bedroom floor and my legs don't work.

There are practical decisions to be made – this might all be my fault – I try to work out what to do.

Everyone else is asleep, so it's early and the most important thing is that I don't get into trouble; shouting will get me into trouble and I know what that means. My brain starts offering me self-preservation instructions:

Don't shout.

Sit still. Someone will come. Mam will come. She'll expect you to walk. She might be angry when you don't. Maybe you'll be able to do it when she gets here. Until then you'd better sit still, keep quiet and wait to see what happens.

A lot of things start to happen and I'm puzzled by all of it.

I'm lifted off the bedroom floor.

I'm not ill but I'm being carried by my dad to the doctor's surgery. It's snowing. It might be another day. I don't know.

I'm not ill but I'm wrapped tight in a scratchy, red wool blanket and placed on the floor of the hall in our front porch. Bits of wool get in my mouth. I can't move. There's an ambulance in the field and two ambulance men are plodding up our path. They're old. They look solemn, sad, even, but not unkind. They shake their heads and come towards our front door. We hardly ever use the front door but today it's open and I'm in the hall. In our living room behind me there seem to be more people than usual; I can hear a low buzz of voices. It sounds important.

Maybe this is the next thing; I'm on my own in a green-tiled room with green gowns and masks on hooks by the door and a cot for a bed. I'm not ill but my legs haven't started working and I must stay in the cot. I'm four years old and I am furious about the cot.

I'm in that cot in the green room for a very long time and I have no idea what's going on. I'm definitely not ill and I'm not frightened, though I still can't walk and I'm bored. Every day serious nurses come. They put on the gowns and masks and do jobs. They say things to each other through the masks but not to me. Some of the things they do involve them co-ordinating their movements like dancers as they wash, roll, lift, tuck and smooth me firmly into the cot.

Doctors come. They bend my knees and press my feet. My left foot works. The right one doesn't seem to be mine. They, too, look sad; they, too, talk to each other but not to me. I think I might be a disappointment to them, so on the morning they try again, I move my not-working foot a tiny amount to the side. I'm relieved. I expect them to be pleased with my performance. I expect a nod of approval or a comment that I've done well, but one turns aside, says something quiet to the other and they laugh together. It's a small laugh; one that's for the two of them. It's not for me but it is about me.

I know now that I have failed a test. I performed my little movement for the doctors and it wasn't good enough. It was small and pathetic: that slight twitch to the right, the one thing I could suddenly do, out of all the ranges of movement they asked me to perform, was laughable. When I see the looks the doctors give each other, hear the laugh, I know I am a disappointment to those men. I know I've failed and I am ashamed. Maybe that's the start of searching faces, recognising the flicker of revulsion – that moment when someone looks at my leg and their jaws tighten for a second before they can stop themselves.

Mam and Dad come. They put on the green things and hand me a fat brown envelope filled with drawings and messages from my class. I'm thrilled to be so important. I show them to the nurses because there's no one else; I tell them that all my class has sent them for me. They're not interested.

Another day Mam arrives with a bunch of sweet-peas, so purple and delicious, so sweetly perfect, I am speechless. They are all the same shade of dark purple, a colour so deep I could dive in, swim like a minnow. The smell of them makes me breathe in and hold the perfume inside me. I cannot believe that they are mine. I feel like a new, older person. Someone who matters.

A wonderful thing that comes in with my parents is a brown-paper parcel from Auntie Jo. I have no extended family to speak of: my dad has no siblings or parents, and Mam and her sister were put into an orphanage by her father after their mother died. Mam's sister lives at the other end of the country; we've never met her but she's all we have, and her neatly tied brown-paper parcels are keenly watched for in the days approaching birthdays or Christmas. It's neither of those dates, but a definite Auntie Jo parcel is there and from it emerges garments – a fleecy yellow nightdress with blue ducks on it and a blue dressing gown with pockets and a collar. I've never worn such clothes.

And there's a pair of slippers, the sort of slippers princesses wear. They are the softest pale blue leather with gold piping and they're trimmed with pale blue fur. The fact that I can't walk in them is a shock and a dreadful disappointment. I step with my left foot and all is good. Then I step with my right foot but as I lift it up it droops and the slipper falls off. I can't stop it. I don't try again. Not to be able to wear the fabulous slippers is too awful, so I put a thick rubber band round the right one to keep it on my dropped foot and I slur it across the lino. It's the start of a lifetime of footwear-related adaptations, failures, embarrassments and occasional thefts from shoe shops.

I dream a dream; maybe it's when I'm in the green-tiled room? Maybe that's when it started? Until I'm sixty-five years old I will keep dreaming the same hot, terrible dream. In the dream I'm on a train – under the train is nothing but water – my body is on fire – someone wearing a grey wool dress is holding me too tight and I can't breathe – she has hold of me and I can't breathe – can't move – can't get away.

When I'm sixty-five I will find out it isn't dream, it's memory.

While I've been shut in the silent room they've been planning how they'll fix my not walking. They will fasten metal rods, thick springs, tight straps and buckles with violent, shining teeth to my bad leg. Special shoes will be made by someone at the hospital so that all the equipment can be fixed on. Then the walking will come back.

And it does, though it's never the same. Not at all. There will be no more skimming the earth; I no longer move through the world like a native. My home is in a wild place between a wood and limestone hills; growing things and animals creep relentlessly into our garden so that, except for the rickety wall at the front, there's no real boundary between what's ours and what isn't. The skin of the hills is thin. Nubs of limestone stick through, like earth's bones, and great chunks of it litter the ground. This world belongs to me. I am first people – indigenous. Nothing separates me from it. I own my body, push it through hawthorn hedges, over walls, up trees. There is nothing to stop me.

Now, after polio, my feet are fixed to the ground and I'm looking down. The body I've lived in is gone. My range is limited and, depending on what's being done to me, that limit is sometimes the distance I can hop.

Hopping gets me as far as the small field in front of our house where in summer I sit on a small slab of exposed limestone. There, yellow lady's slipper flowers crawl towards me from the margins and grass is turfy and short. I can worry at these growing edges, peel them away to discover what's underneath – a dusty, greyish powder, ants, various little armoured things, red mites and minute snails. I take to examining whatever I can reach.

When I'm allowed and able, I search for ways to navigate my unreliable landscape, to catch up with the gaggle of brother and sisters who are going where we'd always gone, doing what we'd always done.

Living where we do, getting over gates and walls is an activity we need to be good at if we're to get about. I can't do it properly any more, so I develop a technique in which I climb/ balance/ pivot/ balance/ pivot back/ check/ jump. It's slow, though, and I try to catch up but their heads bob away, their voices carrying back as they move off then disappear. I used to race ahead. Now I'm last.

I'm last in the school sports-day race. The day after it I get home from school to find a box of sweets. They're called Meltis New Berry Fruits. I am immediately suspicious. Mam says they're for me, from the vicar's wife, a present for trying hard on sports day. I'm angry – I hadn't won – I came last. A prize for coming last is completely against the natural order of things. I don't want them. I won't eat them. I will not have anyone feeling sorry for me and I certainly will not say 'Thank you' to the vicar's wife.

My day is shorter than everyone else's because I have to do physio every evening. This means being shouted in half an hour before the others to walk up and down a sloping plank, have my feet pushed up while I try and push back and all manner of other time-consuming activities given to Mam by the physio I go to on Wednesdays and implemented by her every night. It doesn't seem to be doing much good. My leg is still a cold, dead thing attached to me at the hip.

Inside I think I'm safe, though in reality I'm certainly not. Fortunately, we live in a bungalow, so the distance I can fall is limited. Outside I have my walking spells to keep me from falling. The spells are a complex set of rules that include careful calculation of the patterns on the ground, plus relentless counting: I must create a symmetry of patterning with my footsteps and bring about a set of numbers which, cancelled out, equal an even number. Every time the surface changes I must stop one set of counting and begin a new count. If the last set is an odd number, I must hold the odd set in my head and try to cancel it out at some point with another odd set. Ground with no discernible markings doesn't count, and kerbstones and edgings are neutral territory, so the symmetry rule does not apply. I must not step on any piece of ground which is asymmetrical in shape, nor am I allowed to make any manoeuvre that would look like I'm making a manoeuvre to avoid the asymmetrical bit. These last two are particularly relevant when I'm walking on pavements. I always stick to the rules. If I can't make the patterns right it makes me shudder, but I carry on; start the spell again.

Inside and out, the world remains confusing. There are stories, lies, insects, appointments, gates, doctors, tree roots. People cut into my leg again and again, they fix things in it and to it, shove it into horrible ugly things and never say anything to me. How is anyone supposed to make sense of it?

Language starts to become more of a problem. Unreasonably, I connect my horror of certain words to those smiling plastic girls with their white socks and callipers and collecting boxes. They are so marvellously pretty and normal – the only abnormal thing about them is the callipers. They don't limp; their bad legs aren't skinny and purple with cold. The words applied to me did not apply to them. Some of those words still make me shudder. I call them 'snake words' – they're dangerous. *Disabled* has been one for most of my life. *Cripple* is worse. It has taken me a lifetime to think it and write it.

There were others. Although I knew I limped, I never knew I *hobbled*. Someone at school said, 'We wouldn't have won if you hadn't hobbled round and scored that half a rounder.' I was so shocked I couldn't speak.

There are other things – worse things – I can't talk about. Now, though, I can write most of my snake words. I do it to shock people, including myself, though I've never said any of them aloud in public, except when reading one of my own poems.

Am I addressing the question, why does walking matter?

I doubt it. I'm trying at least to keep to the subject. The things I'm telling you now are as accurate as I can make them, but on another day the story might not be exactly the same.

I'm learning a lot from hospitals and schools about living and moving in the world. I learn that it's not only ironwork and hobbling that attract attention. As my chubby child's body begins to change, I realise that it can be moulded and disguised, the ugly bit covered up. I can make it into something normal – desirable – something people want to possess, not reject. I learn that I can change the shape even more with diet and exercise and clothe it in a certain way and move it in a certain way and make men want it.

It makes me laugh at how easy it is. I can step a fraction closer than necessary in conversation, move a tiny amount, dance in ways that say, *Look, look, everyone, isn't this a beautiful thing!* and change a man's behaviour. I can make him laugh approvingly at my outrageous flirting, make him blush uncomfortably, make him think about sex and what it would be like to touch my body. It's fun. More than that, it makes me powerful. I do not care what it does to anyone else. When I make their eyelids narrow and their lips part, when they're flustered and don't know what to do, I know that I am in control. Sometimes I do it more: make them squirm; keep pressing buttons, not letting them off the hook.

It was also punishment; I wanted them to feel embarrassed and vulnerable. I did it for a few years until I didn't need or want it any longer. I should feel some sense of shame about my younger self's manipulating, mercenary behaviour and the problems I created for other people but, honestly, I don't think I do.

By the time I'm in my mid-twenties I do not need to conjure a sense of power for my body to be good enough as it is. I don't know when this happens.

But I do. Now I've written it, I do know when it happened.

I am just turned twenty-three, on my own in a club in town. A man is watching me. I can't be bothered with performance; it's late and I'm tired. I take a quick glance – at shoulders, clothes, flowing auburn hair, and suddenly I can be bothered. Soon, I move into his flat but in spite of how much we like each other, however much we laugh and however good the sex is, I dread him seeing my leg in the cold light of day. A few months later I'm in the bath. He always makes sure I have as much privacy as I need, but today he comes quietly into the bathroom, lifts my damaged leg from the water, washes it gently and carefully, rinses away the soap then lowers it back below the surface and leaves.

That act was, I think, part of my learning to let go of the need to conjure a sense of power and control: it was when I started to understand that it was possible for my body to be good enough.

As I've grown older the old horrors have almost ceased to matter.

Almost.

Have I made much progress? I'm not sure. I think perhaps the most valuable thing I've learnt is that it really is not my fault. I know that I am as good as other people, that I am acceptable. When I'm exposed at the swimming pool and I know someone is staring, I still shudder but I remind myself that it is not my fault.

The world, however, continues to try to tell me it is: it seems to me to have grown steadily and relentlessly less tolerant of any perceived imperfection. Social media is more vitriolic about people's appearance; more writers produce books with ecstatic accounts of the joy and peace they've found in the simple, natural act of walking; more glowingly healthy fell-walkers in quietly expensive walking gear stride the small screen; more gorgeous TV presenters pose for carefully curated drone shots while explaining the universe/ the construction of some ancient Egyptian tomb/ the rise of *Homo sapiens*.

Those aerial shots probably aren't your idea but here's what I think: all you presenters – you can be as lovely as you like, I'm fine with it, but please stop the sweeping, *look at magnificent me getting out there and doing it* shots. And you writers: be ecstatic, heal yourselves good and proper, but don't tell us that walking and nature are cures.

Don't. Tell. Us.

You damage us with your carefully crafted appearance, your luminous phrases and your tales of redemption through walking. If I could make all of you walk a mile in my shoes – our shoes – I would.

And I'll tell you something else: I think you're kidding yourselves. I think all the gloss, the glory, the loveliness are part of an illusion. I think it starts with fear – of our bodies, of being like us – then you let that fear become fact. 'Fact' that if you walk far enough, fast enough, you can outpace infirmity. 'Fact' that if you can climb enough peaks, you can beat illness. 'Fact' that if you keep at it, keep pushing on, pushing through, you won't need to face what you know is going to happen to you, too.

We are the fault, the flaw, the crack in your armour – in order to believe the illusion, it's necessary for it to be a 'fact' that those of us who claim we can't escape the limitations of our own bodies simply aren't trying hard enough.

As I wrote those last paragraphs I realised something awful and possibly true – that we who are the target of the world's rejection and disgust too often believe these 'facts' the most fervently. Maybe that's what they're for? Because if we believe you, you don't have to believe us.

Does walking matter? Probably, but not in the ways you think.

Notes

A Partial History of Walking with Pain

1. Dorothy Wordsworth, Reading Text of 'Excursion up Scawfell Pike', ed. Paul Westover https://romantic-circles.org/editions.2022.DW.SP-reading.html
2. Maria Jane Jewsbury, quoted in *Dorothy Wordsworth's Rydal Journals*, ed. by Nicholas Mason and Susanne Sutton (Liverpool University Press, 2025), p. 71.
3. Millicent Garrett Fawcett, *Some Eminent Women of Our Time* (London: MacMillan and Co., 1889), p. 176; John Campbell Shairp (ed.), *Recollections of a Tour Made in Scotland* (New York: G. P. Putnam's, 1874).
4. Dorothy misses a year off her age here.
5. *Rydal Journals*, pp. 513–14.

Walking through Time

1. 'First look as new Palace Hotel tours reveal secret and hidden rooms' by Denise Evans (*Manchester Evening News*, 6 September 2016).
2. 'Manchester, cotton and slavery', Manchester Science and Industry Museum website.
3. 'Cotton Capital: how slavery made Manchester the world's first industrial city' by Matthew Stallard, visuals:

David Blood and Lydia McMullan (*Guardian*, 3 April 2023).

4. *Manchester and Abraham Lincoln* by F. Hourani (R. Aitman & Son, printers, 1900).
5. 'How William Gladstone defended his father's role in slavery', by Jonathan Smith and Paul Lashmar (*Guardian*, 19 August 2023).

Symperilambano

1. The reconstructed theatre was opened in 1997. It was the dream vision of actor Sam Wanamaker.
2. In The Bridge production the roles of Titania and Oberon were reversed. The line is usually 'My fairy lord...'
3. Though Shakespeare could not have known these woods personally, as they belonged to the Crown.
4. Four years later, in 1660, theatre was restored and Davenant, along with Thomas Killigrew, was granted a royal patent to produce drama in London, which gave them an effective monopoly that held sway for around 200 years.

Biographies

Kerri Andrews

Kerri Andrews is a writer, editor, academic and a walker, and is director of creative writing at University College, Cork. She is the author of *Wanderers: A History of Women Walking* and *Way Makers: An Anthology of Women's Writing about Walking*. Her edition of *Nan Shepherd's Correspondence* was longlisted for the Saltire Research Book of the Year, 2024. Her most recent book, *Pathfinding: On Walking and Motherhood*, was published in 2025 by Elliott and Thompson and has been long listed for the Highland Book Prize. She has written for the *Guardian*, *Trail* magazine, *The Great Outdoors* magazine, *History Today* and *Scottish Wildlife*. Kerri is based in the Scottish Borders.

Josie Giles

Harry Josephine Giles is a writer and performer from Orkney, living in Leith. Her latest book is the poetry collection *Them!* (Picador, 2024). Her verse novel *Deep*

Wheel Orcadia (Picador, 2021) won the 2022 Arthur C. Clarke Award for science fiction book of the year. Her poetry collections *The Games* (Out-Spoken Press, 2018) and *Tonguit* (Freight Books, 2015) were between them shortlisted for the Forward Prize for Best First Collection, the Saltire Prize and the Edwin Morgan Poetry Award. Her stage show of her poetry sequence *Drone* toured internationally in 2019, and the performance of *Deep Wheel Orcadia* toured in 2025. She has a PhD in Creative Writing from the University of Stirling.

Polly Atkin

Polly Atkin is a poet and nonfiction writer whose work focuses on nature, place and disability. Her poetry collections are *Basic Nest Architecture* (Seren, 2017), *Much With Body* (Seren 2021), and *Emergency Dream* (Seren, 2026). Her nonfiction includes *Recovering Dorothy: The Hidden Life of Dorothy Wordsworth* (Saraband, 2021), *Some Of Us Just Fall: On Nature and Not Getting Better* (Sceptre, 2023 and Unnamed, 2024), *The Company of Owls* (Elliott and Thompson, 2024 and Milkweed, 2026), and *Swimming The Seasons: A Freshwater Almanac* (Saraband, 2026). She works as a freelancer from her home in Grasmere, where she co-owns Sam Read Bookseller.

Gail Simmons

Gail Simmons is known as a 'walking writer'. With a journalism career spanning a quarter of a century, she has contributed numerous travel features to UK and international newspapers and magazines. Her first sole-authored book, *The Country of Larks: A Chiltern Journey*, was published by Bradt in 2019 and was shortlisted for the Edward Stanford Travel Writing Awards. Her second book, *Between the Chalk and the Sea*, which follows a rediscovered pilgrimage route in southern England, was published in 2023 by Headline (Hachette). Gail lectured on the MA in nature and travel writing at Bath Spa University and currently teaches creative non-fiction at Cambridge University.

Anita Sethi

Dr Anita Sethi was born in Manchester and is an award-winning writer and author of *I Belong Here: a Journey Along the Backbone of Britain* which won a Books Are My Bag award and was nominated for the Wainwright Prize for Nature Writing, the Great Outdoors Award and Royal Society of Literature's Ondaatje Prize for outstanding books evoking 'the spirit of a place'. *I Belong Here* was praised as a 'thing of beauty' by the *Sunday Times* and selected as Stanfords Book of the Month, a *Guardian* Highlight of the Year, one of the best travel books by Wanderlust and the *Telegraph*, and Best Travelogue of the

Year by the *Independent*. She has also been published in anthologies including *Women on Nature*, *The Wild Isles*, *Common People*, *Seaside Special* and *We Mark Your Memory: Writing from the Descendants of Indenture*. She has written for the *Guardian*, the *Observer*, *The Sunday Times*, the *TLS* and *BBC Wildlife*, and for BBC Radio 4's *Tweet of the Day* and BBC Radio 3's *The Essay*. She is a fellow of the Royal Geographical Society and a British Academy fellow at the UK's national centre for history.

Beatrice Searle

Beatrice is a writer, artist and inscriptional letter cutter. She is a fine art graduate of Newcastle University, a qualified cathedral stonemason and a former student of the European Lettering Institute in Brugge. In 2017, in a sculptural and performative work called 'For the Journey and Return' she crossed the North Sea by sailing boat and walked 500 miles through Southern Norway on a medieval pilgrim path to Nidaros Cathedral, towing a forty-kilogram Orcadian stone behind her. In 2023, her account of that adventure, *Stone Will Answer*, was published by Harvill Secker. She is a regular speaker at literary festivals and has also written for *Granta*, the magazine of new writing. Beatrice lives in Scotland, in a tiny orchard, with her family and her spaniel.

Katharine Norbury

Katharine Norbury is the author of *The Fish Ladder*, which was shortlisted for the 2016 Wainwright Prize, longlisted for the *Guardian* First Book Award and was a Book of the Year in the *Guardian*, *Telegraph* and *Observer* newspapers. She is the editor of *Women on Nature*, a critically acclaimed anthology of women's writing on the natural world over 700 years in Britain and Ireland. She has contributed to the *Guardian*, the *Telegraph*, *The Washington Post*, *Lonely Planet* and *Caught by the River.*

Anna Fleming

Anna Fleming is a non-fiction writer based in Edinburgh. An active traveller and climber, she collects stories of people, mountains and nature from around the world. Her first book, a nature-writing memoir, *Time on Rock* (Canongate, 2022) was shortlisted for the Wainwright Prize and Boardman Tasker Award. Her PhD with the University of Leeds examined Wordsworth's creativity and Cumbrian communities.

Linda Cracknell

Place, memory and motion are at the heart of Linda Cracknell's writing. A great walker, as reflected in her

2024 book *Doubling Back: Paths trodden in memory*, she also excavates history and myth in fiction with Caithness-set *Call of the Undertow* and *The Other Side of Stone*, which focuses across time on a Perthshire woollen mill. Her latest book, *Sea Marked: Throwing a Line to a Coastal Past*, is a memoir exploring her seafaring ancestry in North Devon. She lives in Scotland and teaches creative writing widely.

Helen Mort

Helen Mort has published three poetry collections with Chatto & Windus. Her memoir *A Line Above The Sky* (on motherhood and mountaineering, Ebury 2023) won the Boardman Tasker Prize and the Grand Prize at Banff, Canada. She is a professor of creative writing at Manchester Metropolitan University and a fellow of the Royal Society of Literature. She lives in Sheffield.

Kate Davis

Kate was born on the Furness Peninsula in Cumbria and still lives there on Walney Island, Barrow-in-Furness. She has always made things and has spent the past thirty years learning about and making poetry. Her poems have been published in a small number of magazines, anthologised in a few more, printed on shopping bags, embroidered on clothes, implanted in benches and remixed by a sound artist. In 2013 she received a Northern Writers' Award and in 2018 her collection, *The Girl Who Forgets How to Walk* was published by Penned in the Margins. It examines her experience of catching paralytic poliomyelitis aged four, and her subsequent relationship with the ground beneath her feet, in particular the limestone landscape where she lives. Kate has developed a performance of poems taken from the book, Julia Parks has made a film of it, and a BBC R4 programme, *Earthbound*, featuring work from the collection was broadcast on 18 September 2020. Her verse novel *Flow* was published by Verve Press in 2025 and she is currently working on a narrative non-fiction book.

Acknowledgements

I have had the best time working on this collection, and I am deeply grateful to all ten contributors for the extraordinary writing they have allowed me to include here. That working on this collection involved going for walks to work through ideas was a delightful bonus.

This collection wouldn't be in existence were it not for the vision and commitment of the team at Batsford Books. Thank you for providing these pieces with such a welcoming home. My particular thanks to Rebecca, Lauren, Mia and Eoghan, but to all those at Batsford who have helped bring this into the world: we couldn't have done it without you.

Thank you as well to my agent, Kay Peddle, who backed this idea from the very beginning.

Finally, to my children, Fhionnlagh and Elisabeth: thank you for showing me a new way forward. The life we are building together fills me with joy, as do you both, every single day. I love you always.